AIR CAMPAIGN

OPERATION *ALLIED FORCE* 1999

NATO's airpower victory in Kosovo

BRIAN D. LASLIE | ILLUSTRATED BY ADAM TOOBY

OSPREY PUBLISHING
Bloomsbury Publishing Plc
Kemp House, Chawley Park, Cumnor Hill, Oxford OX2 9PH, UK
29 Earlsfort Terrace, Dublin 2, Ireland
1385 Broadway, 5th Floor, New York, NY 10018, USA
E-mail: info@ospreypublishing.com
www.ospreypublishing.com

OSPREY is a trademark of Osprey Publishing Ltd

First published in Great Britain in 2024

A catalog record for this book is available from the British Library.

ISBN: PB 9781472860309; eBook 9781472860316;
ePDF 9781472860323; XML 9781472860293

24 25 26 27 28 10 9 8 7 6 5 4 3 2 1

Maps by www.bounford.com
Diagrams by Adam Tooby
3D BEVs by Paul Kime
Index by Fionbar Lyons
Typeset by PDQ Digital Media Solutions, Bungay, UK
Printed and bound in India by Replika Press Private Ltd.

Title page: See caption on p. 91.

Osprey Publishing supports the Woodland Trust, the UK's leading woodland conservation
charity.

To find out more about our authors and books visit www.ospreypublishing.com. Here
you will find extracts, author interviews, details of forthcoming events and the option to
sign up for our newsletter.

CONTENTS

INTRODUCTION

A B-2 Spirit bomber prepares to receive fuel from a KC-135 Stratotanker during a mission in the European theater supporting Operation *Allied Force*. (USAF)

In 1999, the North Atlantic Treaty Organization (NATO) went to war in the skies over the former Yugoslavia, in a campaign remarkable for its purpose and success. The air campaign lasted 78 days, from March to June 1999. Primarily fought by the United States Air Force (USAF), but involving significant multinational air force and naval aviation contributions, the combined allied air armada engaged in a major military air campaign in order to stop Serbian atrocities in Kosovo.

The reason for the air campaign was simple: compel Serbia's president, Slobodan Milosevic to stop the Serbian military's and police forces' massive human rights abuses occurring against ethnic Albanians living in the semi-autonomous province of Kosovo. Milosevic's military and police forces were driving ethnic Albanians from their homes, forcing them to leave the country, and directly murdering them in massacres. NATO's response was primarily a humanitarian one; it acted in defense not of a member state, but in defense of those not capable of defending themselves. One might argue that there were other global incidents where humanitarian intervention was just as necessary, but NATO chose to act here.

Ostensibly, this campaign against Serbia was a NATO-led operation; however, all of the senior level air commanders were from the USAF. Furthermore, the bulk of the air assets came from the United States, including the USAF and the United States Navy. Still, it would be arrogant in the extreme and incorrect for the United States to say these were U.S. Air Force-led operations, because the commitment to this conflict represented a combined opposition among many nations to the genocide occurring inside the borders of Kosovo.

This air campaign proved to be a difficult and complex operation considering the political restraints placed on the air planners. The complex situation they faced proved to be an entirely different scenario from the overwhelming – and relatively quick success – seen during Operation *Desert Storm*. Although created to deal with the threat of a possible Soviet invasion into Western Europe, NATO had adapted as a leader in dealing with global problems, and the ongoing conflicts in the former Yugoslavia were in its backyard. The involvement of NATO into existing Balkan conflicts was part of a larger United Nations operation inside the former Republic of Yugoslavia.

Thousands of ethnic Albanian refugees from Pristina wait 4 April, 1999 at the Macedonian border near the village of Blace for humanitarian aid. (Photo by ERIC FEFERBERG/AFP via Getty Images

From the time of Josip Broz Tito's death in 1980, through the country's fracture and fragmentation in the early 1990s, Yugoslavia broke along the fault lines of race, culture, and religion. With the fall of the Berlin Wall, the opening of travel routes from the Eastern Bloc, and the collapse of the Soviet Union, the people of Yugoslavia also sought their own forms of "*perestroika*" and "*glasnost.*"

The disintegration of Yugoslavia began when Slovenia and Croatia declared independence in June 1991. Macedonia and Bosnia followed suit later the same year. By the mid-1990s, each of the aforementioned countries were independent states, with several other regions declaring autonomy as well. The remnants of these independent nation-states and semi-autonomous regions of the former Republic of Yugoslavia now included only Serbia, Kosovo, Vojvodina, and Montenegro under the presidency of Slobodan Milosevic.

Serbian police and military forces routinely clashed with members of the Kosovo Liberation Army. Here Serb forces sweep the village of Studencane near Suva Reka. Serbian forces claimed they were engaged in operations against a terrorist organization, but the wider world quickly discovered otherwise as news of atrocities began to leak out of Kosovo. (Joel Robine/AFP via Getty Images)

Sea power was an important component of NATO operations during the conflict. In addition to the American USS *Theodore Roosevelt* and the Royal Navy's HMS *Invincible*, the Government of France sent the *Foch*. From her decks a number of strikes were launched against targets in Serbia by Super Étendards. (GERARD JULIEN/AFP via Getty Images)

Milosevic's military arm during the conflicts to come was the Yugoslav People's Army, the *Jugoslovenska narodna armija* (JNA). The JNA fought to bring the breakaway countries back into the former Yugoslavia, although the Serbian leaders and the JNA viewed them not as countries at all, but as rebellious districts. The effort to bring them back was to no avail.

The JNA, ethnic Serbians, Bosnians, and Croatians began a decade-long conflict as one side sought to reassert dominance and the other for independence and global recognition. The conflicts were among the worst seen on the European Continent since World War II. Mass murder, rape, burning of cities, and the forced relocation of civilians all became hallmarks of the "Balkan conflicts." The conflict and violence quickly popularized a term that corresponded with the ongoing genocide: ethnic cleansing.

Into the conflict descended United Nations Protection Forces (UNPROFOR), and for the first time since its creation, NATO entered into a military conflict. NATO leaders, the USAF, and the militaries of the other allied nations began to plan for an air campaign and to accomplish tasks that proved different from the conflicts in which they had previously participated earlier in the decade.

The Balkan conflicts of the 1990s

Operation *Deny Flight*, *Deliberate Force*, and *Allied Force* were a few of the major NATO operations that occurred in the region throughout the 1990s. Collectively known as the

"Balkan conflicts" in America and Western Europe, the engagements highlighted both the successes that followed up the impressive role air power had played in Operation *Desert Storm* in 1991, as well as a growing technological gap between the United States, France, Germany, Great Britain, and some of the other NATO allies.

The former Federal People's Republic of Yugoslavia and later the Socialist Federal Republic of Yugoslavia had begun its slow disintegration after the death of Marshal Josip Broz Tito in 1980. Tito had been the glue that held the multinational and multiethnic regime together. His death simply accelerated the union's dissolution. Six republics, modeled on the Soviet Union, composed the original Republic of Yugoslavia at its demise: Bosnia and Herzegovina, Croatia, Macedonia, Montenegro, Serbia, and Slovenia. Furthermore, there were the two "autonomous" republics of Vojvodina and Kosovo. To call Yugoslavia ethnically, religiously, or linguistically diverse was a massive understatement. Slavs, Serbs, Romani, Sephardic and Ashkenazi Jews, Macedonians, Albanians, Croats, Bulgarians, Bosniaks, and Yugoslavs were all part of the ethnic mixture. It was this diversity, or rather the conflicts between this diversity, which led to NATO's involvement in the country during the 1990s.

Slovenia and Croatia were the first to declare independence. In response, Serbia dispatched the Army of Yugoslavia (JNA) to its borders. Although Slovenia forced a JNA withdrawal, the war in Croatia dragged on for four years. This proved to be the opening salvo in conflicts that would stretch for a decade as the new Federal Republic of Yugoslavia (FRY) – now just Serbia and Montenegro – attempted to maintain some form of control over the breakaway independent nations.

In March 1992, Bosnia and Herzegovina held an independence referendum. Bosnian and Herzegovinian Muslims supported the independence movement, but the ethnic Serbs in the region actively boycotted and opposed the movement. Although the independence referendum passed, war broke out in April between the Muslim factions and the Serbs backed

The "ethnic cleansing" by Serbian forces quickly evolved into a humanitarian crisis of enormous proportions. This photo was taken at the refugee camp in Blace, where thousands of Kosovar refugees fled. (Photo by Yannis Kontos/ Sygma via Getty Images)

HUNGARY

CROATIA

VOJVODINA

NOVI SAD

Ruma

Šabac

BELGRADE

ROMANIA

BOSNIA AND
HERZEGOVINA

SARAJEVO

SERBIA

Niš

MONTENEGRO

PODGORICA

KOSOVO

PRISTINA

BULGARIA

Adriatic Sea

SKOPJE

N

ALBANIA

MACEDONIA

0   50 miles

0   50km

by the Serbian JNA. To make matters worse, ethnic Croats turned on the ethnic Muslims. By August, news and images had leaked of ethnic cleansing and mass rapes by the Serbian forces. In response, NATO launched airstrikes against the JNA in Bosnia: Operations *Deny Flight* and *Deliberate Force*. These operations eventually allowed for a peace deal as part of the Dayton Accords in November 1995.

However, peace in the region was short lived. Ethnic Albanians living in the semi-autonomous region of Kosovo in southern Serbia sought independence in what quickly developed into the crisis of 1998. Again, ethnic and genocidal killings by the JNA forced NATO into action. Between November 1998 and March 1999, the Organization for Security and Co-operation in Europe (OSCE) placed into Kosovo the Kosovo Verification Mission (KVM). Neither Serbian forces, both military and police, nor the Kosovo Liberation Army (KLA) paid particular attention to the OSCE members. Serbian state forces continued to attack ethnic Albanians in Kosovo, and members of the KLA continued to attack members of the Serbian state forces. This eventually led to the NATO intervention and Operation *Allied Force*.

Operation *Allied Force* began as a means to force President Slobodan Milosevic to stop the ethnic cleansing he had ordered in Kosovo. More than 20 years later, there remains a dearth of written histories concerning NATO's air war over Serbia and Kosovo, especially accessible histories that deal primarily with combat operations. Air operations began on March 24, 1999. On that night, NATO forces commenced an air campaign against Serbia in order to put an end to human rights violations that the Serbian Army were executing against the ethnic Albanian population in Kosovo. Some in the media, government, and military circles believed the operation was intended to be a 72-hour operation; in reality, the operation, code-named *Allied Force*, ended 78 days later when Yugoslavia's president, Slobodan Milosevic, capitulated and began withdrawing his forces, the Serbian Army, from Kosovo.

The United States and its allied partners conducted training exercises, including the Red Flag exercise at Nellis Air Force Base in Nevada. The landscape there closely resembled the environment found in Operation *Desert Storm*. However *Allied Force* was going to prove much more problematic than many of the existing training exercises. The bombing of Serbia provided another useful example of how differences between strategy and tactics no longer mattered and how air power had become the preferred tool of Western nations to accomplish political goals. F-117s flying early in the conflict struck underground command and control bunkers, military barracks, radio relay stations, and other targets of both strategic and tactical significance. Each target, regardless of its nature, was just something that needed to be destroyed or disabled and moved NATO closer to ending the campaign. The B-2 bomber also saw its first combat missions during *Allied Force*, flying from its home station at Whiteman AFB in Missouri and returning to base without landing. The combat search and rescue (CSAR) missions provided an excellent case study of just how much realistic training was important to actual operations. The type of training necessary to perform the CSAR mission was far more important than the types of technologies used in the actual rescues. Although CSAR operations were an important task during Vietnam, *Allied Force* set a precedent for how to carry them out effectively.

During *Allied Force*, many aircrews found themselves launching from Aviano Air Base in Italy. This was especially hard for the units already stationed there, as they conducted a mission and then returned home to their families. For the crews who were overseas but were not "downrange," the pilots had to juggle combat operations and their families at the same time, a most unusual occurrence in combat operations.

CHRONOLOGY

1980

May 4 Josip Broz Tito, President of Yugoslavia, dies of complications due to gangrene at the University Medical Centre, Ljubljana.

1991

June 25 Parliaments of Slovenia and Croatia declare independence. The Serbian Army (JNA) deploys.

April 3 JNA withdraws from Slovenia.

1992

March Bosnia and Herzegovina hold an independence referendum.

April Conflict breaks out between Bosnia's Muslims, Croats, and Bosnian Serbs during the independence movement.

April 2 The siege of Sarajevo begins. Both the Yugoslav People's Army and the Army of the Republic of Srpska lay siege to the city. In the end, 13,952 people are killed during the siege, including 5,434 civilians. The siege does not end until 1996, making it the longest siege of a capital city in modern times.

August Ethnic cleansing images released to the public.

1995

July Bosnian Serb forces take over the UN-protected "safe area" of Srebrenica in eastern Bosnia and massacre up to 8,000 Muslim men and boys.

August After the fall of Srebrenica and the bombing of a Sarajevo market in which 41 people are killed, NATO unleashes airstrikes on Bosnian Serb positions as part of Operation *Deliberate Force*.

November 21 A peace deal is signed in the U.S. town of Dayton, Ohio, between Bosnia, Croatia, and Serbia. This becomes known as the Dayton Peace Accords.

December NATO deploys peacekeeping force in Bosnia.

1998

January 8 The "Contact Group" – composed of representatives from the United States, Great Britain, Germany, France, Italy, and Russia – demands a ceasefire, the withdrawal of Yugoslav and Serbian forces from Kosovo, the return of refugees, and unlimited access for international monitors.

February 28 Serbian forces begin first major offensive, killing 24.

March 5–7 The second Serbian offensive begins. This time, 60 Kosovar Albanians are killed.

March 9 The Contact Group again calls for Milosevic's forces to leave Kosovo within ten days.

Late March In the southern Serbian province of Kosovo, fighting breaks out between ethnic Albanian rebels and the JNA.

March 31 United Nations Security Council passes Resolution 1160 and places an embargo on the Federal Republic of Yugoslavia.

May 15–18 Milosevic meets with Ibrahim Rugova, a Kosovar Albanian leader, and the Contact Group agrees to review Milosevic's assets previously frozen, but only if he agrees to continue talks with representatives of Kosovo.

June 15 Air forces of NATO conduct exercise *Determined Falcon* over Albania and Macedonia, just a few miles from the Serbian borders. Thirteen NATO members and 85 aircraft participate.

June 23 American diplomat Richard Holbrooke, special envoy to the Balkans, meets with Milosevic in Belgrade and Pristina; Milosevic makes concession toward UN observers.

July 18 Serbian forces launch another offensive, forcing thousands of Kosovars to depart their homes as refugees. This is the beginning of operations that will eventually force over 300,000 Kosovars from their homes in the coming year.

September 30 UN Security Council Resolution 1199 is passed. It demands "…that all parties, groups and individuals immediately cease hostilities and maintain a ceasefire in Kosovo. Demands further that the Federal Republic of Yugoslavia, in addition to the measures called for under resolution 1160 (1998), implement immediately the measures towards achieving a political solution to the situation in Kosovo as contained in the Contact Group statement of 12 June 1998."

October 5 Special Envoy Holbrooke holds further, and longer, missions with Milosevic.

October 8 NATO ambassadors approve plan for air campaign against Serbia.

October 13 Although NATO issues order to prepare for airstrikes, Milosevic agrees to comply with UN Resolution 1199.

October 24–27 UN Security Council passes Resolution 1203 and encourages both sides to implement the Holbrooke–Milosevic Agreement. Meanwhile, General Wesley Clark meets with General Klaus Naumann to discuss removal of Serbian military and police forces from Kosovo. NATO forces stand down.

December 24 On Christmas Eve, Serbian and Yugoslav forces assault the town of Podujevo, in clear violation of the Holbrooke–Milosevic Agreement, breaking the fragile truce that had held for two months.

1999

January 15 The Racak massacre occurs, resulting in the deaths of 45 Kosovar Albanians including women, children, and the elderly.

February 6–March 23 Peace negotiations occur at Rambouillet, Paris, and Belgrade. No agreement is reached. Special Envoy Richard Holbrooke departs Belgrade. NATO Secretary General Javier Solana orders Supreme Allied Commander Europe, General Wesley Clark, to begin airstrikes.

March 20 The Organization for Security and Co-operation in Europe (OSCE) removes the members of the Kosovo Verification Mission (KVM) from Kosovo after repeated violations by both the KLA and the Serbian government forces, citing a "steady deterioration in the security situation."

March 24 NATO launches air campaign, with the goal of crippling the Serbian war machine in Kosovo. Serbian Army deploys.

March 24–25 USAF F-15C piloted by Lt Col Cesar Rodriguez shoots down a Serbian MiG-29. This is his third confirmed kill following two during Operation *Desert Storm*. Later that night, Capt. Mike Shower shoots down another MiG-29. Royal Netherlands Air Force F-16AM shoots down a MiG-29.

March 25 Captain Jeff Hwang shoots down two MiG-29s.

March 26 Suva Reka massacre occurs. Serbian forces kill 48 Albanian Kosovars including children.

A C-17 Globemaster III from Charleston Air Force Base, South Carolina, arriving from Ramstein Air Base, Germany, offloads U.S. Army personnel at Tirana airfield, Albania. (USAF)

March 27 A U.S. F-117 Nighthawk stealth fighter, piloted by Lt Col Dale Zelko, is shot down near Belgrade. The commander of the missile site, Zoltan Dani, uses the Isayev S-125 "Neva-M" (NATO designation SA-3 Goa) to shoot down the F-117. American combat search and rescue forces rescue Zelko later that night.

March 28 Izbica massacre occurs. Another 93 Kosovars are murdered.

April 1 Serbian forces capture three U.S. service members in the Former Yugoslav Republic of Macedonia. The soldiers – Sergeant Ramirez, 24, of Los Angeles; Sergeant Christopher J. Stone, 25, of Smiths Creek, Michigan, and Specialist Gonzales, 22, of Huntsville, Texas – are captured while on patrol along the border between Kosovo and Macedonia.

April 3 NATO cruise missiles strike targets in the city of Belgrade including the Interior Ministry.

April 12 and 14 NATO airstrikes hit a train, killing 20 civilians. Two days later, on the 14th, NATO bombs a Kosovar Refugee Convoy, killing 73.

April 21 AH-64 Apache gunships arrive in Albania as part of Task Force Hawk.

April 23–25 NATO summit in Washington DC.

April 27–28 At least 377 Kosovar Albanians are murdered during the Meja massacre; 36 are under the age of 18.

April 30–May 1 Reverend Jesse Jackson meets with captured U.S. service members, then with Slobodan Milosevic, and secures the soldiers' release.

May 1 Forty-seven bus passengers are killed when NATO bombs a bridge in Kosovo.

May 2 The three American soldiers captured on April 1 are released after Reverend Jesse Jackson leads an unofficial and non-sanctioned effort.

May 2 Lt Col David Goldfein, commander of the 555th Fighter Squadron and future chief of staff of the USAF, is shot down by a Serbian surface to air missile. CSRA forces rescue him.

May 3 F-117s drop CBU-94s on five transformer yards, cutting electricity to 70 percent of Serbia.

May 5 NATO suffers its first losses when the two-man crew of a U.S. Apache attack helicopter die in a crash in Albania.

May 6 Western powers and Russia announce they have reached agreement over a strategy to resolve the conflict. Russian support is critical to ensure Milosevic's capitulation.

May 7–8 An American B-2 Spirit accidently bombs the Chinese Embassy in Belgrade; three people are killed in the attack. NATO calls this a "tragic mistake."

May 18 and 23 President Bill Clinton says he no longer rules out "other military options," indicating the possibility of a NATO and American invasion of Kosovo.

May 23 In a final escalatory step, NATO forces begin striking the Serbian power grid.

May 25 The North Atlantic Council approves an expansion of the Kosovo Force (KFOR) to 48,000. The following day the Kosovo Liberation Army goes on the offensive.

May 27 The UN War Crimes Tribunal indicts Slobodan Milosevic for his "crimes against humanity." The indictment comes from the International Criminal Tribunal for the former Yugoslavia (ICTY).

June 2 Slobodan Milosevic agrees to end the conflict.

June 10 NATO suspends airstrikes, effectively ending NATO's air campaign against Serbia.

June 12 Russian forces depart Belgrade and enter Kosovo. They seize Pristina Airport. Three hours later KFOR arrives.

2006
March 11 Slobodan Milosevic dies of a heart attack in his cell at the UN War Crimes Tribunal detention center. He had been on trial for war crimes since 2002. He was posthumously found guilty in numerous verdicts of being a member of a criminal enterprise and guilty of the crimes of persecution, murder, deportation, and inhumane acts.

ATTACKER'S CAPABILITIES

NATO's air power on display

Significantly smaller than the massive Operation *Desert Storm*, the NATO-led air war against Serbia was nevertheless a dominant display of almost total aerial supremacy. However, NATO was facing a disciplined and well-organized enemy much more effective at countering NATO's capabilities than were the Iraqi forces led by Saddam Hussein.

Campaign planners had the weight of NATO air assets behind them. Thirteen countries contributed aircraft. The United States eventually committed 639 aircraft, with the other NATO members contributing an additional 277 for a total of 916. The general officer who would oversee this aerial armada was Lieutenant General Michael Short. Short's – rather turgid – official title was "commander, Allied Air Forces Southern Europe and Stabilization Forces Air Component, Naples, Italy, and commander, 16th Air Force and 16th Air and Space Expeditionary Task Force, U.S. Air Forces in Europe, Aviano Air Base, Italy." His career had spanned just about every fighter and attack aircraft the USAF had to offer. During his career, Short had flown the A-7, A-10, F-4C/D/E, F-15E, F-16C, F-102, F-106, F-117, and RF-4C, and had accumulated over 4,600 hours in these aircraft.

During one interview with the media Lt Gen Short pointed out:

I don't think there's any doubt in the Serbs' mind about our ability to use airpower. They were clearly witnessing in August and September 1995 our selective and precise airpower to bring about a specific result, it's important that anyone who would see themselves as potential adversaries of the NATO alliance that they see we were a very fine air force in 95 and 98… we're a whole lot better now.

There was one problem with Lieutenant General Short's statement. Yugoslav forces had in fact observed NATO's air actions during Operation *Deliberate Force*. These forces had also observed American and allied successes during Operation *Desert Storm* and had extensively worked out countermeasures to NATO's air superiority.

A two-seat version of the F-15, the F-15E variant was called the "Strike Eagle." This version was made with air-to-ground operations in mind, including close air support, interdiction, and other attack missions. A USAF weapons system operator, commonly called the "WZO" (pronounced wizzo) sat behind the pilot. Here are two F-15Es from the 494th Fighter Squadron, RAF Lakenheath, United Kingdom. (Jeffrey Allen/ USAF/Getty Images)

Operation *Allied Force* was truly a combined NATO effort, with aircraft from more than a dozen countries participating, including this Turkish F-16C seen refueling from an American KC-135R Stratotanker. Note that the Turkish F-16C is carrying AIM-120s on the outboard wings and AIM-9 missiles under the wing, indicating an air-to-air patrol mission. (USAF/Getty Images)

Chain of command

Any discussion of NATO operations must begin with the organization's chain of command. At the very top of the NATO structure sits the North Atlantic Council (NAC), the principal decision-making body for the organization. All permanent members of NATO have a seat on the NAC, and the Secretary General of NATO chairs the Council. In 1999, the Secretary General of NATO was Spain's Javier Solana. Reporting to the NAC was the NATO Military Committee, headed by the Chair of the NATO Military Committee. General Klaus Naumann of Germany held the post from 1996 until May 6, 1999, when the office was taken over by Admiral Guido Venturoni of Italy. Throughout the conflict, the NAC granted Secretary General Solana the authority necessary to begin, prosecute, and end the air campaign. Finally, under the NATO Military Committee was the actual military organizational commands of NATO.

The military command structure of NATO begins with the Supreme Headquarters Allied Powers Europe (SHAPE), headed by the Supreme Allied Commander Europe (SACEUR). During the *Allied Force* operations, United States Army General Wesley Clark held this post. Clark was also "dual-hatted" as the Commander-in-Chief, United States European Command (CINC EUCOM). Along the United States lines, Clark had a senior U.S. Air Force officer, General John P. Jumper, who was the head of the United States Air Forces in Europe (USAFE). Although General Clark headed the military organization as SACEUR, he still reported to NATO's Military Committee, composed of the Chiefs of Defence of NATO member countries.

The overall commander of NATO operations for *Allied Force* was U.S. Navy Admiral James O. Ellis, who was both the Commander, Allied Forces Southern Europe and Commander, U.S. Naval Forces Europe. Ellis also held operational control (OPCON) over Allied Strike Forces, Southern Europe (STRKFORSOUTH), and the Allied Air Forces, Southern Europe (AIRSOUTH). Under Admiral Ellis as commander of AIRSOUTH, came Lieutenant General Short, the Commander Allied Air Forces Southern Europe, and the Combined Force Air Component Commander (CFACC). In his role as both AIRSOUTH and CFACC, Lt Gen Short and his amassed staff of air planners set about planning and directing all NATO air component operations for all contributing forces' members. Also problematic was that

General Wesley K. Clark, a West Point Graduate and Rhodes Scholar, served as both the Commander-in-Chief, United States European Command and as the Supreme Allied Commander Europe of NATO from 1997 to 2000. (U.S. Army)

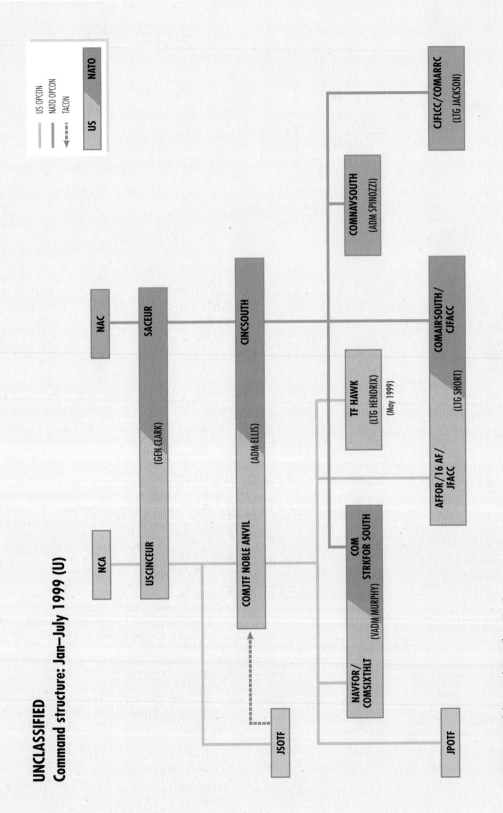

UNCLASSIFIED
Command structure: Jan–July 1999 (U)

Legend:
- US OPCON
- NATO OPCON
- TACON
- US
- NATO

NAC

SACEUR (GEN CLARK)

NCA

USCINCEUR (GEN CLARK)

CINCSOUTH (ADM ELLIS)

COMNAVSOUTH (ADM SPINOZZI)

CJFLCC/COMARRC (LTG JACKSON)

COMJTF NOBLE ANVIL (ADM ELLIS)

TF HAWK (LTG HENDRIX) (May 1999)

COMAIRSOUTH/CJFACC (LTG SHORT)

AFFOR/16 AF/JFACC

COM STRKFOR SOUTH

NAVFOR/COMSIXTHLT (VADM MURPHY)

JSOTF

JPOTF

NOTE: Does not include Joint Task Force "Shining Hope"
UNCLASSIFIED

NATO was in the throes of a post-Cold War reorganization. If all of the above was not confusing enough, while NATO called the entirety of the operation *Allied Force*, the United States chose for inexplicable reasons to call it Operation *Noble Anvil*.

One of the problems throughout *Allied Force* was the nature in which the United States allowed air assets to operate. General Jumper as USAFE maintained operational control of the B-1, B-52, and B-2 bomber force as well as the F-117 stealth fighters. Although Lt Gen Short had tactical control over these aircraft, they did not run through any NATO reporting lines. All other aircraft were under the operational control of Admiral Ellis and the tactical control of Lt Gen Short and did report through the NATO chain.

NATO's massive air arm

The NATO activation order for the campaign that became *Allied Force* came on October 13, 1998. While the diplomatic talks at Rambouillet continued, air assets from the various nations began to move toward the Balkans. Perhaps nowhere was this more noticeable than at Aviano Air Base in Italy, where six F-15Es from the 494th Fighter Squadron[1] of the 48th Fighter Wing arrived in December; the 492nd Fighter Squadron swapped out with the 494th

One way in which NATO forces clearly outmatched the Yugoslav Air Force was in the possession of low-observable or stealth aircraft. While not invisible, these aircraft were extremely difficult to detect by radar. NATO leaders felt the stealth fighter and bombers provided an advantage that the Serbians could not counter, but they were proven mistaken in this regard. (USAF)

1   A note on squadrons. Some NATO countries, including the United States, typically convert a squadron to an "expeditionary squadron" upon deployment. Thus, the 493rd Fighter Squadron becomes the 493rd Expeditionary Fighter Squadron upon landing at a foreign base. For simplicity's sake, I have chosen to drop the expeditionary from the nomenclature for ease of reading and narrative flow.

To keep control of the aerial situation and to vector fighters toward enemy aircraft NATO employed the E-3 sentry, more commonly known as the AWACS for its role, Airborne Warning and Control System. (USAF/ Getty Images)

in January. Aviano already claimed several Portuguese F-16s, Spanish F/A-18s, and RAF fighters and E-3D Airborne Warning and Control System (AWACS). Landing just behind the F-15Es were 15 A-10 Thunderbolt attack aircraft of the 81st Fighter Squadron, although most fliers and members of the Air Force called the A-10 the Warthog, or just the hog. On February 21, the F-117s from the 8th Fighter Squadron, 49th Fighter Wing, Holloman Air Force Base, New Mexico, arrived to add their low-observability stealth technology to the growing air armada. Over the coming weeks, even more aircraft landed at Aviano, including F-16CJs from the 23rd Fighter Squadron.

Cervia Air Base was another Italian base near the Adriatic, but located at the top of Italy's boot, what could be called the Italian Peninsula's "calf." There, the U.S. landed F-15Cs of the 493rd Fighter Squadron as part of the 501st Operations Group from Lakenheath Air Base in England. The F-117 was not the only low-observable stealth aircraft used during the campaign, but it was the only one stationed in theater; the B-2 Spirit launched and returned to Whiteman Air Force Base for all of its missions. One of the other U.S. bombers, the B-52, departed its stateside bases for RAF Fairford. F-15C and F-16C air-to-air fighters, F-16CJ specializing in the suppression of enemy air defense (SEAD), F-15E Strike Eagles, A-10 for close air support and attack missions, all moved to bases in Italy or Germany. EA-6Bs provided electronic warfare and were the only jammers available to American aircrews. EA-6Bs typically carried the air-to-ground missile (AGM-88) high speed anti-radiation missile (HARM) as well as the AN/ALQ-99 electronic countermeasure (ECM) pod.

In total, 13 NATO nations sent aircraft to be a part of the coalition. Poland, Hungary, the Czech Republic the newest NATO members and Greece, Iceland, and Luxembourg were the six nations that did not participate. Next to the United States, France and the United

The Royal Air Force was a large contributor of air power to *Allied Force*. Here an E-3D sentry AWACS is seen alongside two Panavia Tornado F3s. (Photo by Adrian Pingstone, Public Domain)

Kingdom contributed the most aircraft numerically. France and the UK were also the only other nations capable of employing precision-guided munitions (PGMs), thus allowing them to participate in more strike missions, especially once rules of engagement began to tighten as the campaign dragged on. The German Luftwaffe, although only bringing 14 Tornados to the operation, would participate in a number of SEAD missions. Although Germany and Italy were two of the nations not equipped with PGMs, their Tornado IDS (interdictor/strike) and ECR (electronic combat reconnaissance) did employ the AGM-88 HARM, essentially a precision-guided missile, as long as the enemy

radar remained turned on and radiating. The AGM-88 had the ability to home in on electronic transmissions coming from surface-to-air radar systems. Other NATO members sent various Mirage, Jaguar, and Tornado aircraft. There were also NATO E-3 AWACs, air-to-air refuelers. This was the most modern air armada ever assembled.

Over the course of the winter of 1998 and into 1999, NATO members continued to funnel air power into Italy and closer to the Balkans in anticipation of what was rapidly becoming probable airstrikes. Following their performance in Operation *Deliberate Force*, the German Luftwaffe returned to play a part in *Allied Force*, deploying Tornado ECRs and IDSs to Piacenza Air Base. The French Air Force (ALA) landed eight Mirage 2000Cs, four Mirage 2000Ds, and four Jaguar As at Istrana Air Base in northwest Italy near Venice on the Adriatic Sea. Over at Gioia del Colle Air Base, near the heel of the "boot," the RAF moved four Harrier GR7s and a Canberra PR9 reconnaissance aircraft. Amazingly, the Italian Air

Having just completed aerial refueling, a French Air Force Mirage 2000C moves away from a USAF KC-135R Stratotanker and heads for a combat patrol mission during Operation *Allied Force*. (USAF)

Gioia del Colle Air Base was home to numerous allied fighters during the entirety of *Allied Force*. The base was located on the heel of Italy's boot, on the Adriatic sea directly across from the Balkans. Here maintenance personnel of the Italian Air Force prep a Tornado for operations on the first day of combat operations, March 25, 1999. (GERARD JULIEN/AFP via Getty Images)

Force continued to operate the venerable F-104s. This U.S.-built aircraft gained the moniker "the missile with the man in it" back in the 1960s, but was still an acceptable Combat Air Patrol (CAP) platform capable of air-to-air combat and intercepts.

While this book focuses primarily on combat operations and combat aircraft, not a single strike would have taken place were it not for the global reach of air mobility assets of the various NATO members. This included cargo aircraft as well as air-to-air refuelers that maintained the crucial "air bridge" that allowed combat air power to virtually surround the country of Serbia. Included in the cargo aircraft was the United States' newest air mobility asset, the C-17 Globemaster III. A total of 120 C-17s moved assets from the United States and around the European continent before, during, and after combat operations. Since the C-17 was designed from the beginning to be an inter-theater strategic airlifter, but also with the capability to land at smaller and less-established airfields, the C-17 had the capability to bring its cargo directly to smaller air bases and bypass the need to land, offload cargo, and reload it onto a smaller aircraft such as the C-130 Hercules.

Overcrowding at Aviano eventually forced a dispersal of NATO aircraft to other bases, including Gioia del Colle, but no sooner did one unit depart than another arrived.

Contribution by country and mission area							
	Fighter/Attack/Strike Fighter	Bomber	Attack Helicopter	CSAR	Tanker	Cargo/ Transport	AWACS/EW
United States	F-16CJ F-117 F-14 F-15C F-15E A-10 F/A18 F-14 AV-8B	B-52 B-1B B-2A	AH-64	MC-130 MH-53 MH-60	KC-135 KC-10	C-130 C-17 C-5	E-3 EC-130 ABCCC EA-6B
Belgium	12x F-16						
Canada	18x CF-18						
France	12x Jaguar, 3x Mirage IV-P, 6x Mirage F1 CR, 8x Mirage 2000C, 8x Mirage 2000D, 4x Étendard IVP, 4x Super Étendard		4x Super Frelon		3x KC-135	1x C-160	1x E-3F SCDA
Germany	14x Tornado					1x C-160	
Italy	22x Tornado ECR/IDS, 6x AMX, 6x F-104 ASA				1x 707T		
Netherlands	18x F-16				2x KDC-10		
Norway	6x F-16					1x C-130	
Portugal	3x F-16						
Spain	6x EF-18				1x KC-130, 1x CASA 212		
Turkey	11x F-16						
United Kingdom	16x Harrier GR7, 1x Canberra PR9, 12x Tornado, 7x Sea Harrier FA2		10x Sea King		3x VC-10	4x L-1011	2x E-3D

Combat aircraft and mission areas		
Country	Aircraft	Mission area
United States		
	F-16CJ	SEAD
	F-117	Precision attack/bombing
	F-14	Precision strike
	F/A-18	Air superiority/precision strike
	F-15C	Air superiority
	F-15E	Precision strike
	B-1B	Precision bomber
	B-2A	Precision attack/bombing
	B-52	Precision and area bombardment
	A-10	Close air support
	AV-8B	Close air support
France		
	Jaguar	Attack
	Mirage IVP	Attack
	Mirage F1 CR	Fighter/attack
	Mirage 2000C/D	Multirole
	Étendard IVP	Reconnaissance
	Super Étendard	Strike
Germany		
	Tornado	Multirole
Italy		
	Tornado ECR/IDS	Electronic warfare/interdiction strike
	AMX	Ground-attack
	F-104 ASA	Combat air patrol and interceptor
Netherlands		
	F-16	Air superiority
Portugal		
	F-16	Multirole
Spain		
	EF-18	Multirole
Turkey		
	F-16	Multirole
United Kingdom		
	Harrier GR7	Interdiction/close air support
	Sea Harrier FA2	Interdiction/close air support
	Tornado	Multirole

Naval forces

NATO forces also held complete control of the sea lines of communication and brought from that domain a significant amount of air power in its own right. The U.S. Navy's USS *Theodore Roosevelt* and its various squadrons operated out of the Mediterranean. The *Theodore Roosevelt* was the fourth carrier of the Cold War-era Nimitz class and in service since 1986. The *Roosevelt* alone had more aircraft and firepower than the entirety of the Yugoslav Air Force. Embarked upon the USS *Theodore Roosevelt* was Carrier Air Wing Eight (CVW-8). Under CVW-8 were the VF-41 Black Aces, VF-14 Tophatters, VFA-15 Valions, VFA-87 Golden Warriors, VAQ-141 Shadowhawks, providing electronic countermeasures, and early warning aircraft from the VAW-124 Bear Aces.

The Royal Navy brought HMS *Invincible* to the fight, here photographed off the coast of Cyprus on April 13, 1999. A veteran of the Falklands War, *Deny Flight*, and *Deliberate Force*, the "Vince" carried a complement of Sea King helicopters that conducted humanitarian operations and FA2 Sea Harriers for strike operations. (Crown Copyright Reserved/AFP via Getty Images)

Although a longstanding foreign policy tool of the United States, when the air campaign began, there was not a U.S. Navy aircraft carrier in the theater. The USS *Theodore Roosevelt* had to be rerouted and make a return trip to the Adriatic in order to participate, but only arrived a week after the air campaign began, arriving on April 7. The same was true for the British aircraft carrier HMS *Invincible* that arrived April 11. At the beginning of the operation, only two Navy destroyers, the USS *Kearsage* (LHD-3), carrying AV-8B Harrier IIs of the U.S. Marine Corps' VMA-231, and U.S. submarines were on station. The French aircraft carrier *Foch*, with its 16 Super Étendards and four Étendard IVPs, was already in the Adriatic Sea and ready to conduct operations.

Arriving in relatively short order was the Royal Navy's HMS *Invincible* (R05). The *Invincible* was the first – and namesake – for a class of light aircraft carrier of the British Royal Navy. The "Vince," as it was known to its crew, carried a complement of between 12 to 18 Harrier GR7/9 and between four and 12 Sea King ASaC and Merlin HM MK 1 helicopters. During the coming conflict, the carrier's FA2 Sea Harriers provided protection for NATO air forces, while its helicopters supported the aid program to refugees during the height of the crisis. The Sea Harrier FA2 entered service relatively recently, joining the fleet in 1993, and many of the pilots on the *Invincible* had previous deployment experience to Bosnia in 1994. The FA2 featured the Blue Vixen radar, which, at the time, was known as one of the most advanced "pulse Doppler" radars used on any military aircraft. The FA2 also carried the AIM-120 AMRAAM (advanced medium-range air-to-air missile). The final newly built Sea Harrier FA2s were delivered on January 18, 1999. In addition to the HMS *Invincible*, the following ships were allotted to *Allied Force* operations from the Royal Navy: HMS *Newcastle*, a Type 42 destroyer; HMS *Iron Duke*, a Type 23 frigate; HMS *Grafton*, also a Type 23 frigate; HMS *Splendid*, a hunter-killer submarine; and the support ships RFA *Fort Austin* and RFA *Bayleaf*.

Training

There is no doubt that that the United States led the way in terms of the amount of time committed to realistic training, but coalition partners also participated in large force training events. Since the end of American involvement in the Vietnam conflict, the United States air and ground forces had fundamentally reshaped how they trained for operations. In terms of the air arms, both the U.S. Navy and USAF had either created or completely revamped their Fighter Weapons Schools. Both had created a dedicated cadre of "Aggressor" aircraft to train their weapons officers in the ways of Soviet-style tactics. The USAF's Red Flag exercise became the global standard for training for combat in both service, joint, and multinational operations. NATO allies had routinely flown to Nellis Air Force base in Nevada to participate in the Red Flag exercise. Operation *Desert Storm* clearly demonstrated the benefit of the exercise for coalition operations. Furthermore, some U.S. aircrews had either flown or trained against actual Soviet MiG-17, MiG-21, MiG-23 – and in all probability MiG-29 – aircraft as part of the top-secret *Constant Peg* program.

Although there were clearly differences in capabilities between the Allied nations – most notably the United States and their NATO allies – each of the participating countries had spent decades training together of anticipation of the perceived conflict with the now defunct Soviet Union, so in terms of compatibility, although there were going to be problems, the countries were well aware of each other's capabilities and abilities. The results of Operation *Allied Force* only reinforced the importance of joint and allied doctrine, interoperability training, and tactics, techniques, and procedures.

Deck crew of the *Roosevelt* give an F/A-18 a final look before the aircraft launches on a sortie on April 12, 1999. (DOD)

Intelligence, surveillance, and reconnaissance

Another key difference between NATO and Yugoslav forces was in intelligence, surveillance, and reconnaissance (ISR). Beyond satellite imagery, which flowed into the NATO military command from partner nations, some of the most advanced ISR aerial capabilities flew in support of *Allied Force*. This included the unmanned RQ-1 Predator, which provided tactical-level real-time observation of targets on the ground. The RC-135V/W provided on-scene intelligence collection, analysis, and dissemination. The U-2 Dragon Lady of the United States was the high-flying collector of photographs and images. The E-8 joint surveillance and targeting attack radar system (JSTARS) was an airborne command-and-control system designed to detect and track moving targets. ISR assets from other NATO nations included: CL-289 drones and Crécerelle unmanned aerial vehicles from France, and the Hawker Siddeley Nimrod from the RAF.

Although typically not thought of as an ISR asset, the Navy's F-14 Tomcats did come equipped with the TARPS (tactical air reconnaissance pod system), which provided imagery and aided in near real-time transitioning of aircraft in flight to high-value and time-sensitive targets. This 17ft, 1,850lb pod carried three cameras and produced 3,350ft of reconnaissance images.

An F-14 Tomcat returns from a strike mission aboard USS *Theodore Roosevelt* (Cvn-71). (U.S. Navy/Getty Images)

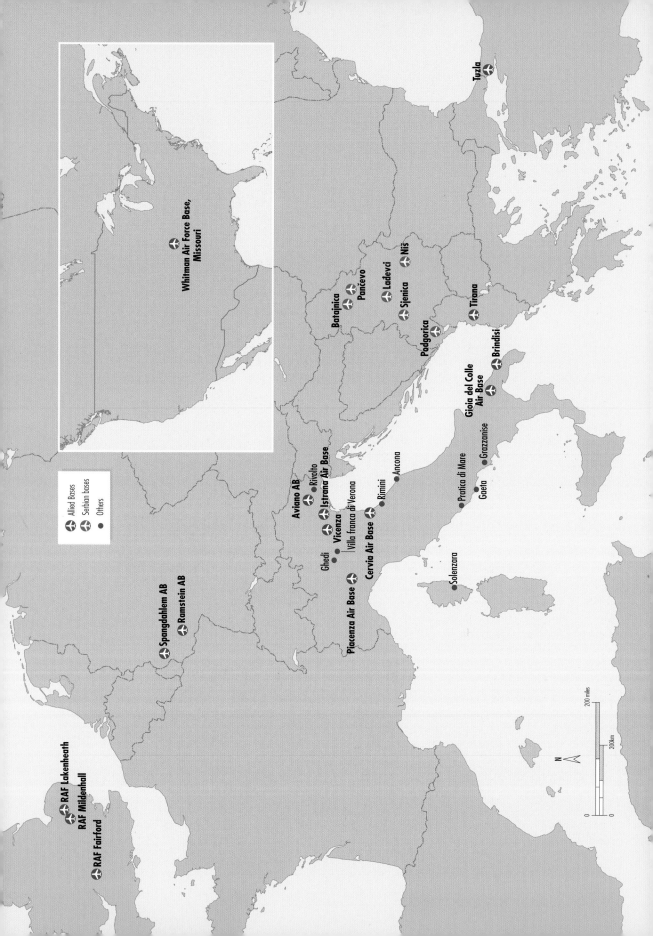

OPPOSITE NATO BASES IN ALLIED FORCE

Space

Space operations played an increasingly important role after Operation *Desert Storm* and reached new levels during the combat operations in the Balkans. *Allied Force* saw the first use of the joint direct attack munitions (JDAMS). "Dumb bombs" were outfitted with a global positioning system (GPS) guided kit that drastically increased the accuracy of these munitions. Although *Desert Storm* is sometimes referred to as the first "space war," *Allied Force* saw these operations reach a new level of maturity.

After *Desert Storm*, the importance of space-based information was fully apparent, and the number of space-based assets was undergoing exponential growth. Although quaint by today's standards, space-based communications, data-transfer, imaging, and video-teleconferencing remained novel concepts being exploited in ways never before used in warfare. However, there was a downside to all of this technological wonder. A truism of all combat, but of air power in particular, has always been "centralized control, but decentralized execution." For the first time, commanders had real-time influence over ongoing battlefield operations and even, at times, direct access to aircraft in flight. Future leaders would be forced to grapple and guard against their ability and desire for too much access to operations.

Combat search and rescue

A final important contribution to the NATO air arm was the ability to perform combat search and rescue (CSAR): picking up downed aviators in isolated and dangerous enemy territory. Inside military circles, this was known as personnel recovery (PR).

Air Force combat search and rescue operations dated to World War II but had really reached a new level of persistence during the Vietnam conflict. Since 1976 these CSAR missions proved to be a mainstay of Air Force exercises and real-world operations. Outside of Red Flag, those select pilots chosen to attend Fighter Weapons School were also exposed to training for CSAR operations, particularly A-10 pilots. Lieutenant Colonel Chris Haave stated in his book *A-10s Over Kosovo* (2003) that graduates of the weapons school became qualified to lead CSAR missions and that CSAR-qualified airmen ranked at the top of U.S. and NATO "must have capabilities" when planning for combat. CSAR-qualified commanders were given the coveted call sign of "Sandys," which had lineage tied to rescue efforts during Vietnam. Lieutenant Colonel Haave stated that "Due to the difficulty and complexity of the mission, only the most experienced and capable A-10 pilots are selected to train as Sandys." Training to lead a CSAR mission was among the most mentally challenging for pilots, but would be needed during *Allied Force*.

CSAR missions were conducted by Air Force special operators known as pararescue jumpers. Pararescue jumpers, or "PJs," as they were commonly called, practiced at their home stations, at exercises, and in real-world operations. More than any other mission type, the training conducted to pick up a downed pilot in hostile territory was tested during *Allied Force*. The training proved worth it. The realistic training exercises used A-10s and rotary wing assets to rescue downed personnel. Between 1980 and 1990, the annual Close Air Support Red Flag and the classes on command and control taught at the A-10 weapons school changed the way

The venerable A-10 Thunderbolt II, more commonly called the "Warthog," was a tank-killing machine and an invaluable weapon for close air support and as on-scene commanders during combat search and rescue operations. (DOD)

An A-10 normally based at Pope AFB, North Carolina, but deployed in support of operations in Kosovo, made an emergency landing at Petrovec Airport in Macedonia. Note that one of the aircraft's engines has been removed as maintenance personnel work on the jet. (Jack Guez/AFP via Getty Images)

the Air Force conducted rescue operations. Never before had Air Force personnel and assets been able to conduct a rescue operation in such a highly contested threat environment as the one found in Serbia.

The United States Air Force headquartered its CSAR assets out of San Vito dei Normanni Air Station, more commonly called Brindisi, the city located near the base on the heel of Italy and on the coast of the Adriatic. At Brindisi sat MC-130H Combat Talon IIs from the 67th and 9th Special Operations Squadrons, MH-53J Pave Lows of the 352nd Special Operations Group (SOG) and 21st Special Operations Squadron. Other CSAR assets arrived from the United States, including four MH-53Ms of the 20th Special Operations Squadron and four MH-53Gs from the 55th Special Operations Squadron. All of these could also be "forward deployed" to Tuzla, Bosnia and Herzegovina.

CSAR operations were an important component of the overall allied war effort. Any pilots shot down could rely on the knowledge that every effort was going to be made to send in a rescue force and pick them up. According to Colonel Whitcomb's book *On a Steel Horse I Ride: The History of the MH-53 Pave Low in War and Peace*, the United States Air Force had nine MH-53 and four MH-60G helicopters assigned the CSAR responsibility during the coming operation. These aircraft could be launched at a moment's notice. During *Allied Force* two American airmen owed their rescue to the CSAR forces: Lieutenant Colonel Dale Zelko, an F-117 pilot shot down on March 27, 1999, and Lieutenant Colonel David Goldfein, an F-16CJ pilot and squadron commander shot down on May 2, 1999.

"Boots on the ground"

Often forgotten in the tally of the attacker's capabilities were the forces on the ground of the Kosovo Liberation Army. The mantra of no "boots on the ground" echoed by United Nations and political leaders around NATO, including U.S. President Bill Clinton, meant that the forces on the ground fighting for their very existence against the Serbian Army were often ignored then as now. The KLA was a militia composed of ethnic Albanians and ranging in size from a force of 12,000 troops to over 45,000 troops depending on the source and time. In all likelihood, the KLA had roughly 20,000 soldiers during the *Allied Force* portion of the Kosovo War.

The RV I PVO did use its Soko J-22 Orao against the forces of the Kosovo Liberation Army. (Srđan Popović/CC-BY-SA-4.0)

DEFENDER'S CAPABILITIES

A capable threat

NATO forces were certainly not going up against a "peer" competitor, but this should not be taken as an indication that the Serbian forces would be defeated easily. Serbian forces consisted of only a handful of modern aircraft, including MiG-29s. However, they did possess a very formidable integrated air defense system (IADS) composed of radar systems, AA artillery, and surface-to-air missiles (SAMs). Their surface-to-air capabilities not only included more than 100 SAM launchers, but they were staffed by a cadre of officers who had observed American and allied tactics during *Desert Storm* and other air operations in the Balkans and who were well prepared to go against NATO forces. The weapons, doctrine, and tactics were of a Soviet design and training, but they were also adaptable and innovative. The Yugoslav forces' "game plan" could best be described as "survival in the face of overwhelming force."

A report issued to the United States Congress after the war noted that in the face of NATO's combined strength, Milosevic chose to fight through indirect means rather than through direct confrontation. He used "terror tactics against Kosovar civilians; attempts to exploit the premium the alliance placed on minimizing civilian casualties and collateral damage; creation of enormous refugee flows to trigger a humanitarian crisis; and the conduct of disinformation and propaganda campaigns."

In addition, with Serbia essentially having the "home field advantage," several other factors aided in its defensive operations, including weather, terrain, and logistics. Allied forces were going to have to contend with a country whose topography can best be described as rugged and at worst as nearly impenetrable. The entire country south of the capital city of Belgrade was composed of hills, valleys, and four separate mountain systems: the Dinaric Alps, the Carpathian, Balkan, and the Rila-Rhodope mountains. A near constant cloud cover over the southern half of the country also certainly aided the defenders against air attacks. Finally, the former socialist republic had strong backing from Russia.

MiG-21bis composed the bulk of the RV I PVO although they did not fly a single combat sortie during combat operations against their homeland. Military leaders felt they were too vulnerable and outmatched by NATO air power. (Srđan Popović/ CC-BY-SA-4.0)

An S-125 NEVA (NATO SA-3 Goa) from the 250th Air Defense Brigade. A missile just like these on display brought down an American F-117 on the third night of operations. (Srdan Popović/CC-BY-SA-4.0)

Army of Yugoslavia (JNA)

Since Serbia was a part of what remained of the Federal Republic of Yugoslavia, both "Yugoslav" and "Serbian" were often used interchangeably to describe the military forces in the coming conflict. Serbian ground power was made up of a mix of infantry, motorized, and mechanized forces. Although varying wildly by source, the JNA's total force structure included 115,000 soldiers, over 20,000 police forces, 1,250 tanks, and 800 armored personnel carriers. The tanks included a mix of Soviet-era T-72 main battle tanks, older T-54 and T-55s, and M-84s: Yugoslav copies of the T-72. A number of the forces above were actively involved in ethnic cleansing operations before the beginning of hostilities. Inside Kosovo, as many as 40,000 Yugoslav and Serbian forces conducted operations against the ethnic Albanians. Before hostilities began, NATO estimated that as many as 700,000 ethnic Albanians had already been forcibly displaced by Milosevic's forces.

Air Force of Yugoslavia

Properly the name for the opposing air force was the Yugoslav Air Force, *Ratno vazduhoplovstvo i protivvazdušna odbrana* and abbreviated as the RV I PVO. However, it was also commonly known as the Air Force of Serbia and Montenegro. This often causes confusion for readers and researchers as the two are often used interchangeably in the same way as the Yugoslav/Serbian ground forces. There were two elements to the RV I PVO: an air corps and an air defense corps. In January 1999, the RV I PVO began planning its defensive operations should NATO begin airstrikes. Defense of the Serbian homeland focused on two major sectors: the fielded forces operating in Kosovo and the capital city of Belgrade.

Serbian air power, while not the size of Iraq's, was still composed of fairly modern Russian-built aircraft, although how many of them were flyable was open to debate. Their frontline fighter was the MiG-29 of which they only had 16. In addition, they also had older Vietnam and Cold War era MiG-21s, numbering 64 in total, although these played very little role in the coming conflict. However, it was in the area of air defense assets that the NATO allies held the most concern for Serbian and Yugoslav abilities – in particular the surface-to-air missile threat (SAM).

Serbian air defense

Serbian air defenses posed a more significant threat than did their air-to-air fighters. This included three SA-2 battalions and 16 SA-3 battalions, both of which were supported by Low Blow fire control radars (FCRs). They also had five SA-6 regiments – roughly 25 SA-6 batteries – supported by Straight Flush FCRs. In addition to these fixed assets, there were roughly 100 SA-9 and SA-13 vehicle-mounted missiles and man-portable shoulder-launched infrared missiles (MANPADs). Finally, 1,850 pieces of 27mm and 57mm anti-aircraft artillery were active in the field. One hundred acquisitions and tracking radars, plus an unknown number of Serbian operatives loitering outside of NATO air bases and monitoring take-off times of Allied aircraft, gave Serbian radar operators advance warning and accurate timing to turn on their radars to track incoming Allied aircraft. When combined with Serbia and Kosovo's relatively small size – roughly the size of England and smaller than the U.S. state of South Carolina – this meant that Serbia's IADS was among the most densely packed in the world.

A special note is worth mentioning here. Serbian air defense operators were among the best in the world as they would rapidly prove in the opening days of the conflict when they showed they had the capability to track and engage the United States' "silver bullet" weapon: the low-observable F-117 Nighthawk. The F-117 had flown unopposed in the skies over Iraq, but would not be able to do so over Serbia, due to the efforts and ability of the Serbian air defense operators.

Their ability to track the low-observable stealth aircraft was also due to the observers Serbia had outside of the NATO air bases. At Aviano, Serbian observers had been monitoring NATO air activity, including training sorties. Inside Serbian air space the Yugoslav 280th Electronic Intelligence Centre also collected valuable information as the NATO aircraft operated in nearby training orbits.

Since Serbia's overall operational plan was simply to survive NATO airstrikes, Serbian air defense forces maintained a robust dispersal plan as well as limiting radar emissions. This allowed for the survivability of the air defense surface-to-air missiles and the radar sites. This alone seriously hindered NATO air operations in the coming campaign.

P-18 radar (NATO Spoon Rest-D). A Soviet-designed radar and exported around the world, the P-18 was instrumental in helping Serbian missile crews down American aircraft. (ShinePhantom/CC-BY-SA-3.0)

Yugoslav/Serbian Air Force by aircraft type, function, and numbers			
83rd Fighter Regiment	123rd Fighter Squadron 124th Fighter Squadron	MiG-21bis/UM	Pristina
204th Fighter Regiment	126th Fighter Squadron 127th Fighter Squadron	MiG-21bis/UM MiG-29/UM	Batajnica
172nd Aviation Brigade	239 Fighter Bomber Squadron 242 Fighter Bomber Squadron	G-4 Super Galeb J-21 Jastreb J-22 Orao	Golubovci
98th FB Aviation Regiment	241st Fighter Bomber Squadron	J-22 Orao	Nis Air Base
119th Helicopter Regiment		Mi-8	Nis
250th Air Defence Missile Brigade	SA-3		Belgrade
240th Air Defence Regiment	2K12 Kub (SA-6)		Mobile
20th Air Surveillance Battalion			Stara Pazova and Kacarevo

One of the biggest problems facing NATO forces was the number of Serbian forces actively operating inside the border of Kosovo. This included as many as 14,000 soldiers of the

The Integrated Air Defense System

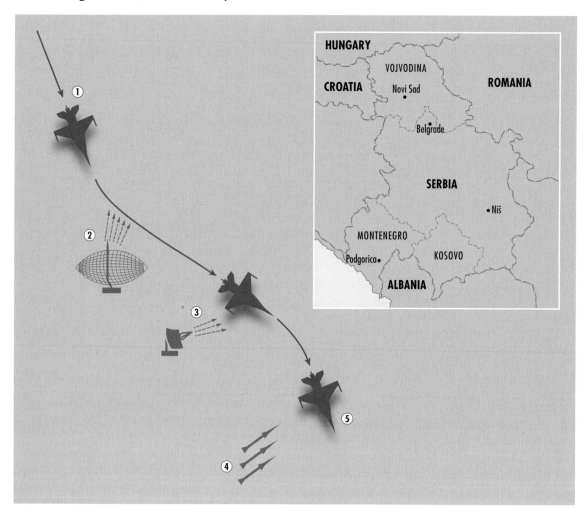

Serbia's Integrated Air Defense System was active throughout the country, but was especially dense around the cites of Novi Sad, Belgrade, Niš, and Podgorica (in Montenegro).

1. Observers on the ground near American and NATO bases watch Allied aircraft as they take off. This information is relayed to Serbian air defense forces.
2. Long-range Soviet-era early warning radars including the P-14 (NATO "Tall King") or the P-40 (NATO "Long Track") detect incoming strike aircraft.
3. This information is then passed along to missile operators using the SNR-125 (NATO "Low Blow") fire control (FCR) radars.
4. SAMs launch against strikers.
5. NATO countermeasures include EA-6B for radar jamming or EA-6Bs and F-16s carrying AGM-88 HARMs.

OPPOSITE SERBIA'S IADS SYSTEM

JNA, 200 armored personnel carriers (APC), and 200 tanks. In addition, Milosevic had at his disposal another 10,000 police force members inside Kosovo. There were also hundreds of mortar and artillery pieces well ensconced inside Kosovo. These troops and police were stationed throughout Kosovo. The police forces had six regional headquarters, and the JNA had artillery, armored, and mechanized brigades throughout the province. The Kosovo Liberation Army held only a fraction of the entire region centered in Kosovo and around the towns of Lapusnik and Malisevo.

Camouflage and concealment

Another avenue the Serbian forces used extensively to their own advancement was deception operations. Serbian forces made extensive use of camouflage and concealment as well as decoys to fluster and frustrate allied operations. Since Serbia's overarching plan called for simply surviving NATO air attacks and preserving its force, it did not matter that camouflage and concealment hindered movement and maneuver. One might argue that motorized and mechanized forces have become a hallmark of the Western way of war, and it certainly frustrated NATO planners that Serbia simply refused to move their forces out in the open.

Serbian forces hid their assets throughout the country. One American report noted that the Serbs "used natural cover such as woods, tunnels and caves, civilian homes and barns, and schools, factories, monasteries, and other large buildings to hide their personnel and weapons." Out in more open areas, Serbians created fake targets that looked like real targets. Using a relatively low-technology counter to NATO's supremacy, Serb forces cobbled together fake anti-aircraft artillery (AAA) sites, vehicles, and SAM sites. Serbia also dispersed its aircraft and moved its real air defense assets, which hindered the NATO SEAD campaign.

On the eve of battle

Shortly before hostilities commenced, Serbian air and missile defense forces began a pre-planned dispersal of forces. This operational deployment not only assured the survivability of aircraft, missiles, and radars, but it also compounded NATO's ability to have a firm grasp on where enemy forces were at the opening of the conflict. From Batajnica and Pristina the Yugoslav Air Force moved MiG-29s and MiG-21bis to four different bases: Nis, Sjenica, Podgorica, Ponikve. These deployments included five of the MiG-29s from the 204th Fighter Regiment, 127th Fighter Squadron to Nis, Ponikve, and Podgorica. Four MiG-21bis moved to each of the dispersal bases. Eight J-22 Oraos from the 252nd Fighter Bomber Squadron and ten Galeb G-4s from the 229th Fighter-Bomber Squadron also dispersed. Transport aircraft moved the maintenance and support personnel needed to operate the aircraft at the deployed locations. Instead of having two principal fighter and bomber bases, the RV I PVO now had six separate bases composed of mixed units to defend Serbian air space.

There is no doubt that Serbian forces knew the opening salvo of the war was imminent. On the afternoon of March 24, Serbian radar detected an increased amount of air activity and noted that multiple AWACS, tankers, and fighters were massing on the borders of Serbia.

The Golubovci Air Base in Montenegro held an underground hardened aircraft shelter that proved to be a tough nut to crack for the NATO attackers. (Photo by MILO-VAN/ Public Domain)

CAMPAIGN OBJECTIVES

A rare view inside the Combined Air and Space Operations Center (CAOC). The CAOC was the hub of all air planning and execution efforts during the operation and served as the "nerve center" for all air activity. This more recent photo of the CAOC clearly shows the multinational nature of the operations floor. (USAF)

NATO's goals

On May 28, 1998, the North Atlantic Council, meeting at the Foreign Minister level, set out NATO's two major objectives with respect to the crisis in Kosovo. The first was to "Help to achieve a peaceful resolution of the crisis by contributing to the response of the international community." The second was to "promote stability and security in neighbouring countries with particular emphasis on Albania and the former Yugoslav Republic of Macedonia."

On October 13, 1998, following a deterioration of the situation, the NATO Council authorized activation orders for airstrikes.

For NATO, there were five stated goals:

1. Ensure a verifiable stop to all military action and the immediate end of violence and repression in Kosovo;
2. Withdrawal from Kosovo of Serbian military, police, and paramilitary forces;
3. Agreement to the stationing in Kosovo of an international military presence;
4. Agreement to the unconditional and safe return of all refugees and displaced persons, and unhindered access to them by humanitarian aid organizations; and
5. Provide credible assurance of Serbian willingness to work on the basis of the Rambouillet Accords in the establishment of a political framework agreement for Kosovo in conformity with international law and the Charter of the United Nations.

President Clinton on March 24 noted:

Our strikes have three objectives: First, to demonstrate the seriousness of NATO's opposition to aggression and its support for peace. Second, to deter President Milosevic from continuing and escalating his attacks on helpless civilians by imposing a price for those attacks. And, third, if necessary, to damage Serbia's capacity to wage war against Kosovo in the future by seriously diminishing its military capability.

President William Jefferson Clinton of the United States talks with President Slobodan Milosevic of Serbia at the Ambassador's Residence in Paris, France, during peace talks in 1995 four years before the events of *Allied Force*. (CIA)

Air campaign planners set about achieving these goals by:
1. Deterring further Serbian attacks against the people of Kosovo;
2. Reducing the ability of the Serbian military forces to continue their offensive operations against the people of Kosovo; and
3. Degrading Serbian air defense systems in order to reduce the risk and threat to NATO aircraft and crews.

Essentially NATO forces operated under a model of three Ds: *demonstrate* resolve and seriousness of NATO intentions, *deter* Slobodan Milosevic in further attacks against the ethnic Albanians in Kosovo, and *damage* the military capability of the Yugoslav/Serbian forces.

For President Slobodan Milosevic, once he realized an attack by NATO air power was imminent, he had only two goals: use his integrated air defense system to punish NATO aircraft, and "outwait" NATO's willingness to continue attacks.

Planning begins

Official planning on what would become *Allied Force* actually began on September 24, 1998. On that date, the NATO defense ministers met at Vilamoura, Portugal to begin discussions on what a possible – even probable at this point – air campaign might look like. During this session, the defense ministers designed the rough outline for two independent air operations and approved the necessary activation warnings.

The first air plan was for a traditional and extended five-phased air operation, to begin with a suppression of enemy air defense (SEAD) campaign and advancing through the phases to destroy or seriously degrade Yugoslav military fielded forces and the security police apparatus.

The second air plan was for a quick-force air attack reaction on short notice, limited in nature, and was to be activated in direct response to an unspecified but serious event or events that occurred inside the borders of Kosovo. This limited-response action eventually found itself integrated into phase one of the air campaign. Perhaps this is why there was so much confusion and conjecture that *Allied Force* was initially envisioned to last only 72 hours.

OPPOSITE MAJOR TARGETS IN SERBIA

The CAOC

NATO air planners at the Combined Air Operations Centre (CAOC) in Vicenza, Italy, used the two approved plans and made continual adjustments over the next six months. The CAOC was the brain of the entire air operation. From here, all signals for movement and action flowed. The U.S. Air Force viewed the entirety of the CAOC as a weapon system in itself. Just like an F-15E has a pilot and weapons system operator working jointly to conduct a mission or a Navy destroyer had a crew working toward a single mission, the CAOC had several hundred members operating in the same manner. Instead of a headquarters, the CAOC more closely resembled the starship *Enterprise* from the Star Trek Series. Just as the *Enterprise* had a bridge where senior leaders kept track of the ship's operations, the CAOC had a battlecab that overlooked the "floor" where operations were monitored. The CAOC was also a gathering place for international partners. On any given day one could find representatives of almost every NATO air force moving about. Land component and maritime component forces were also present.

Located in the same building or in adjoining facilities as the operations floor, the CAOC had five divisions that worked on a 48-hour cycle to plan, assess, monitor, and re-plan each day's strikes. The five divisions were the Strategy Division (SRD), Combat Plans Division (CPD), Combat Operations Division (COD), Air Mobility Division (AMD), and Intelligence, Surveillance, and Reconnaissance Division (ISRD). The five divisions worked jointly to form the overall battle rhythm for air operations.

Javier Solana served as the Secretary General of NATO from 1995 to 1999 and led the alliance during Operation *Allied Force*. (DOD)

The CAOC took ideas, concepts, targets, and plans and turned them into an operational air plan. Targets were turned into a master air attack plan (MAAP), and MAAPs turned into daily missions. Here, at the operational level, air planners took NATO objectives and lists of targets and placed specific aircraft and specific weapons against those targets. The result was the daily air-tasking order (ATO). The ATO was the daily list of missions. It included everything from a unit's specific mission and call sign to aerial de-confliction, timelines, and radio frequencies. All of this was done on an around-the-clock basis. Once the air operation began, the CAOC planners would take the NATO objectives, develop further targets, place aircraft and weapons against these targets in a process called "weaponeering," conduct the day's operations, assess the day's operations, and repeat the process.

After the collapse of negotiations at Rambouillet, the order to begin airstrikes came down through the command structure. On March 23, Secretary General of NATO Javier Solana gave General Clark the order to commence operations. H-Hour for Operation *Allied Force* was set for the following evening, March 24, at 1900hrs Coordinated Universal Time (UTC), 2100hrs in Belgrade, and 1500hrs in Washington, DC.

THE CAMPAIGN

From 72 hours to 78 days

An American B-52H Stratofortress sits on the ramp at RAF Fairford. Munitions personnel prepare to load an AGM-86 air-launched cruise missile (ALCM) into the B-52 one week into the campaign. (USAF/ Getty Images)

Although initially planned – or at least perceived in certain circles – for only 72 hours, the air campaign ended up having three distinct phases. The first phase focused on "rolling back" the Serbian air defense system. After this was successfully accomplished, phase two called for strikes against military targets in Serbia below the 44th parallel and south to the Kosovo border. Finally, phase three ushered in airstrikes against targets north of the 44th parallel, including striking Serbia's capital, Belgrade.

One of the first steps in any air campaign is the selection of targets. All NATO members participating in the air campaign had the capability to nominate targets. All targets flowed from their nation's respective civilian and military intelligence organization into the Joint Target Coordination Board. The Joint Target Coordination Board was co-chaired by Lieutenant General Michael Short and by commander of the 6th Fleet Vice Admiral Daniel J. Murphy, Jr. Short served as both the joint forces air component commander (JFACC) in a strictly U.S. role and also as the air component commander Allied Forces Southern Europe (AFSOUTH). Proposed targets then had to flow "up" the chain of command, first to the Commander-in-Chief, Allied Forces, Southern Europe (AFSOUTH) commander Admiral James Ellis and then to Supreme Allied Commander Europe, U.S. General Wesley Clark. However, even once Clark had vetted and approved the targets, they were then sent to the North Atlantic Council (NAC) and the individual NATO members for final approval. It proved to be a cumbersome process. Since any of the NATO members had the authority to veto a target, the process significantly limited the number of targets.

Since this was at its core a mission to stop a humanitarian crisis, NATO members took extensive steps to ensure that the selected targets were valid military targets. Thus, the rules of engagement for Operation *Allied Force* were extremely restrictive. Two targeting processes emerged, one that flowed along national lines for the United States and one that flowed along NATO lines. As mentioned, NATO targeting proved cumbersome. The United States, Britain, France, Germany, and Italy reviewed each target. Each country also undertook its own legal review. This was further complicated by the fact that very few of the individuals approving the targets were located at the same base or headquarters. Finally, unlike *Desert Storm* where many of the communications nodes, fielded forces, and air bases were in the rural desert, many of the targets in Serbia and Kosovo were in densely populated areas; with the overwhelming desire to limit collateral damage and civilian casualties, this made the approval of targets in urban areas even more difficult. Despite the cumbersome process, NATO planners did eventually streamline the process and greatly increased the approved target list as the conflict dragged on.

President Bill Clinton dines with airmen from the 86th Airlift Wing at Ramstein Air Base, Germany. (DOD)

What was initially meant to be a decisive message-sending three-day conflict turned into an extended 78-day air campaign, in which allied strategic attacks, air-to-air engagements, and the downing and rescue of allied aircrews wrote itself into the history of air power studies. The evolvement into a drawn-out campaign, and the eventual end of the campaign, left a rich history and seemingly endless debate about what air power accomplished and conversely the limits of air power itself.

Prior to the commencement of hostilities, NATO had an approved target list of 50 targets, although a full target list of nearly 170 targets existed. By the end of the campaign, the target list had grown to 979, including air defense assets, communications centers, armament depots, and military storage facilities. At this time NATO's force included 120 U.S. and 100 allied aircraft, although a much smaller number of these would actually operate as "shooters."

A Tomahawk cruise missile launches from the aft missile deck of the USS *Gonzalez* (DDG-66) on March 31, 1999. (DOD)

Three nights begin the campaign

Due to the prolific nature of the Serbian air defense forces, NATO had instituted a 15,000ft "hard deck" that no allied aircraft could go below for the initial strikes. On Wednesday March 24, 1999, shortly after 2000hrs local time in Belgrade (1400hrs on the East Coast of the United States in Washington, DC and 1900hrs Greenwich Meridian Time in London), the air campaign began, but the aircraft participating in the operation had taken to the skies hours earlier.

Before the first aircraft went wheels-up that night or the first cruise missile headed toward its predetermined impact point, an enormously complicated ballet had to be orchestrated. Ingress and egress routes, tanker orbits, holding orbits, and combat air patrol aerial (CAP) racetracks were all set over the Adriatic Sea, Bosnia and Herzegovina, Hungary, and Croatia. NATO planners established altitude de-confliction route launch times, and times over target to decrease the possibility of a midair collision or friendly fire incident. Thanks to international and multi-force exercises between services and coalition partners, many of the pilots had experienced similar training events before, even if not on this scale.

Night one

Early in the morning hours of March 24, two B-2A Spirit stealth bombers of the 509th Bomb Wing launched out of Whiteman Air Force Base, Missouri. The early departure ensured the B-2s would be over Serbia that night to deliver their joint direct attack munitions (JDAM) bombs and then return directly to Whiteman, a 30-hour round trip, a combat world record. While the B-2s did fly alone and not as part of larger strike packages, they did have jamming support from the EA-6Bs, and just in case it was needed, F-16CJ SEAD aircraft orbited nearby.

Across the Atlantic at RAF Fairford, eight B-52Hs of the 2nd Bomb Wing departed around 1045hrs from the cloudy, drizzly air base. Two of the B-52s turned back as un-needed "spares," as the other six members of Havoc flight continued on. The B-52s were known around the globe as the Stratofortress, but everyone who knew and worked with them simply called them the BUFFs (Big Ugly Fat F***ers). These six BUFFs carried AGM-86C air-launched cruise missiles (ALCMS) rather than traditional gravity bombs, giving them the ability to stay well outside of Serbian SAM rings. The B-52s flew south, turning east at Gibraltar, and flew through the Mediterranean and began orbiting in their predetermined area, awaiting nightfall.

In the early evening, with nightfall coming, F-117s, EA-6B Prowlers, and F/A-18 Hornets launched out of Aviano Air Base in Italy. Above the strikers headed toward Serbia and Kosovo, E-3 AWACS monitored the aircraft from their predetermined orbits over Croatia and farther out over the Adriatic Sea. This information also fed directly back to the Combined Air and Space Operations Centre. At other bases across the Italian boot, the NATO allies took to the sky, including the RAF Harriers, Luftwaffe Tornados, French ALA Mirage 2000s, and Royal Norwegian F-16MLUs. All of the strikers were preceded into Serbian air space by a series of cruise missiles launched by the U.S. and Royal Navies operating in the Mediterranean, Adriatic, and Aegean Seas. These sea-launched cruise missiles (SLCMs) shot from their containers and arched into the evening sky from the USS *Gonzales* (DDG-66), USS *Philippine Sea* (CG-58), and the attack submarines USS *Albuquerque* (SSN 706), USS *Miami* (SSN -755), and HMS *Splendid* (S106), headed for their air defense and communications targets. Serbian observers in Italy noted the launch times of the attacking force and early warning radars of the RV I PVO's 280th ELINT unit picked up the incoming armada.

Inside NATO's Combined Air Operations Centre (CAOC) at Vicenza, Italy, the air component commander Lieutenant General Michael Short and hundreds of other NATO

Left to right: Two AIM-120 AMRAAMs and an AGM-88 HARM sit on the wing of a NATO fighter. (DOD)

service members kept an eye on the overall campaign as Operation *Allied Force* began in earnest. In the first night of the planned 72-hour operation, aircraft struck their targets in two "waves," running roughly from 1945hrs local time until 0100hrs, and continuing again from 0100hrs through 0300hrs, now March 25.

The first missiles to reach their targets were the air-launched cruise missiles (ALCMs) and sea-launched cruise missiles (SLCMs). The standoff and long-distance-launched cruise missiles were instrumental in the opening hours and days of the campaign to strike targets

The US F-15C first entered the American inventory in 1975. During Operation *Desert Storm*, the F-15 accounted for 31 shoot-downs of enemy aircraft. *Allied Force* saw that number increase by three. (USAF/Getty Images)

The RNLAF's first aerial victory since World War II

The last time an aircraft from the Royal Netherlands had an air-to-air victory was during World War II. This was about to change with the commencement of NATO operations. On the first night of strikes, a four-ship of F-16Ams, each armed with four AIM-120 AMRAAMs, two external fuel tanks, and a Northrop Grumman ALQ-131 ECM pod, took off from their base to serve as a fighter escort mission to protect one of the first NATO strike packages. After takeoff and an in-flight refueling over the Adriatic Sea, the flight crossed over Albania and flew into Serbia. Shortly after entering Serbian air space, one of the NATO E-3 AWACS informed the flight that three MiG-29 fighter aircraft had taken off from an air base near Belgrade.

The RNLAF F-16s spread out and moved into a "wall" formation. Flying at an altitude of roughly 20,000ft, the F-16s were looking down at the MiGs below them flying at 5,000ft.

The MiG-29s launched from the air base at Batajnica, home of the Yugoslav Air Force's only MiG-29 unit, the 127th Fighter Aviation Squadron, known as the "Knights." The AWACS vectored the four RNLAF F-16AMs toward the threat. As the F-16s approached the MiG-29s, they used their own radars to track and prepare to engage. Only one of the MiGs was picked up by all four F-16s, and once the RNLAF were within a prescribed weapons firing envelope the flight lead, Major Peter Tankink, in F-16A/MLU #J-063, shot one AIM-120 AMRAAM against the MiG. The missile took 30 seconds to travel from the F-16 to the MiG-29. The head-on missile intercept took place 18km from the lead F-16. Ironically, the MiG-29 pilot was attempting to land his aircraft. The missile hit the MiG-29, the pilot ejected, and the RNLAF had its first aerial victory in 55 years.

while NATO knew the air defenses would be at their highest level of alert. As IADS systems were slowly degraded, heavier use of crewed aircraft could be used in the skies over Serbia. Six of the massive B-52Gs launched their AGM-86C air-launched cruise missiles at the electrical power stations and began systematically turning off the lights in certain areas of Serbia. Following these attacks, fixed-wing aircraft primarily from the United States began attacking the radar station at Podgorica and airfields in Serbia, Kosovo, and Montenegro.

The RV I PVO (YAF) was not going to take the attacks without a fight. Although woefully outnumbered in every category – numerically, training-wise, and technologically – MiG-29s took to the sky to defend their air space. On the first night of operations there were two separate air-to-air engagements. At 1950hrs, as the first ALCMs and SLCMs arrived at their targets, Major Iljo Arizanov departed Nis in a MiG-29 (18112), flying to an orbit point over Kosovo between the cities of Djakovica and Suva Reka, north of Prizren. Arizanov would later note many systems on his MiG were unserviceable, including his radio and radar warning. Unbeknownst to Major Arizanov, two separate four-ship flights of F-15Cs from the 493rd Fighter Squadron "Grim Reapers" were already overhead protecting two different strike packages. One flight flew north into Serbia to protect F-117s heading for Belgrade, and the second set was flying a combat air patrol (CAP) over Kosovo.

The second four-ship flight had Arizanov's MiG-29 pegged. As the flight lead and number two focused on a different contact, the number three and four aircraft steadily and methodically tracked Arizanov from 70 miles out, 30 degrees off the F-15's nose, as he flew at 10,000ft. In the number three F-15C, call sign Knife 13, sat Lieutenant Colonel Cesar "Rico" Rodrigeuz, a two-time MiG-killer from *Desert Storm*. Rico directed a climb, dropped his tanks, and "pushed up" his afterburners. At 25 miles, Rico fired one AIM-120. It was only at 15 miles that Arizanov picked up the F-15s visually. Arizanov needed another 30 seconds to be in a weapons firing zone. It was 30 seconds he did not have. On his heads-up display (HUD) Rico watched the missile timer countdown to zero. At that exact moment, a fireball lit up the sky and glared off the snow-covered mountains. Arizanov ejected and spent the next two days evading forces of the Kosovo Liberation Army as he headed back toward Serbia. He was eventually picked up by a JNA unit and made it back to his base at Pristina. Round one went to the Americans.

Meanwhile, the northern group of F-15Cs of the 493rd Grim Reapers, led by Captain Michael "Dozer" Shower, set up two separate CAPs north of Belgrade. Captain Shower, at 37,000ft, committed to engage a MiG-29 (19111) flown by Major Nikolic. Again, the MiG-29's systems were malfunctioning and Nikolic was unaware Captain Shower had him targeted until the first AIM-120 passed by or exploded near his aircraft. By that time, Shower had already released an AIM-7, which also missed due to maneuvering by Nikolic. Shower, now pointed nose-down and at 20,000ft, released a second AIM-120 toward his MiG-29 opponent. This one was guided directly into the rear of Nikolic's aircraft, destroying the aircraft and forcing the major to eject. Unbeknownst to either the MiG or F-15 pilot, an American F-117 was inadvertently caught directly in between this air-to-air engagement. Completely "stealthed-up," the F-117 saw all three of Captain Shower's missiles pass over his cockpit. The two F-15C Eagles from the 493rd Fighter Squadron had engaged and destroyed two Yugoslav MiG-29s from the 127th Fighter Aviation Squadron (the Yugoslav only MiG-29-equipped squadron).

Also that night, a four-ship flight of F-16AMs of the Royal Netherlands Air Force (RNLAF) entered Serbian air space after taking off from Amendola and refueling over the Adriatic Sea. Each F-16AM was equipped that night with four AIM-120 AMRAAMs, external fuel tanks, and the ALQ-131 electronic countermeasures pods. The F-16AMs entered Serbia from the southwest after crossing over Albania. Their mission was to escort a NATO strike package. NATO E-3 AWACS informed the F-16AM that three MiG-29s had just launched from the Belgrade air base Batajnica. One of the MiG-29s that did manage

The burned-out remains of one of the RV I PVO's MiG-29s on the morning after strikes began. On the first night of operations, five MiG-29s took off and three of these were shot down, two by American F-15Cs and one by an F-16 AM of the Royal Netherlands Air Force. (U.S. ARMY/AFP via Getty Images)

to get into the air also had radar and communications problems, another indication that the MiG-29s were far from capable of an equal engagement. The pilot of this MiG-29, Major Milutinovic, was ordered to land at Nis instead of his predetermined Ladjevci. On his way to Nis he was struck by what he thought was ground fire and forced to eject. He had actually been struck by a missile and was lucky to survive. That missile came off the wing of one of the RNLAF F-16s. The RNLAF flight lead, Major Peter Tankink, in F-16A/ MLU #J-063 of the 332nd Squadron, fired an AIM-120 AMRAAM. After a flight time of 30 seconds, the missile impacted and resulted in the first air-to-air victory for the RNLAF since World War II.

Some sources later indicated that at least one of the airborne MiG-29s that night successfully fired an R-73 (NATO AA-10 Alamo) air-to-air missile in an ineffectual counter air response, but given the MiG's radar and avionics problems, this seems unlikely. Interestingly, only five MiG-29s took to the sky that first night, and none of the MiG-21s took to the skies. With regard to the MiG-21s, it was later reported that shortly after hostilities commenced they had been intentionally grounded rather than risk chance encounters with the technologically advanced allied forces. In retrospect, this proved to be the right decision. The MiG-29s that took off that night each had considerable difficulty with their avionics and communications equipment. It is doubtful the even older MiG-21s would have fared any better and would have simply become fodder for allied aircrews searching the night sky for any chance to engage in the age-old art of aerial combat.

While this might seem like a lot of action to open the campaign, in reality, allied air crews only struck about 40 Serbian targets the first night. The first night saw attacks against long-range radar sites, as part of the attacks against the Serbian IADS. The air bases housing the Yugoslav Air Force also felt the weight of the first night's strikes. This included bunker-buster bombs, which penetrated the roofs of hardened aircraft shelters, destroying everything inside, something the RV I PVO was not prepared for. While aircraft could be moved, if the associated support machinery including auxiliary power units (APUs) used to start the aircraft were not also moved, then the aircraft were as effectively grounded as if they had been destroyed. Three command posts, known surface-to-air missile sites, and the headquarters of the 280th ELINT were hit. The first night was meant to significantly degrade the RV I PVO's ability to operate or what one book called "deliver a knockout punch." This did not

Aeritalia F-104S Starfighters operated by the Italian Aeronautica Militare prepare to launch in an air defense role to protect Italian airspace – home to NATO aircraft as well – during the early phase of *Allied Force*. The F-104 S was an authorized production model of the American F-104 Starfighter. (GERARD JULIEN/AFP via Getty Images)

happen. Although the Serbian MiGs would only take to the skies infrequently in the future, the bulk of the Serbian IADs remained intact, and this rapidly had an effect on the conduct of NATO's future missions.

NATO operating as a combined team

The first night of operations saw participation from most of the NATO countries. The Italian Air Force, the Aeronautica Militare Italia (AMI), used its Tornado IDS from the 155 Grupo and its AGM-88 HARM missiles to shoot at Serbian air defense sites. They were joined by the German Luftwaffe, also employing Tornados, but the ECR model.

The first night saw more than 400 sorties and 120 strikes in the opening hours of the campaign. Serbian radars were the primary targets the first night, including a P-14 "Tall King" radar at Kacarevo and other long-range radar sites, limiting Serbia's ability to track future strikes. NATO strikes also began degrading the Yugoslav Air Force's ability to counter any other attacks by striking air bases and the MiGs on the ground. This included using bunker-buster bombs to penetrate hardened aircraft shelters. On the first night, NATO targeted five separate air bases – those at Batajnica, Pristina, Podgorica, Ladjevci, and Ponikve.

The first night, the NATO attacker observed no SA-2 or SA-3 missile launches. Contrary to popular belief that the Serbians were husbanding limited resources of missiles, they were in actuality maintaining strict discipline to ensure the survival of their systems. Having observed the allied attacks during Operation *Desert Storm* and other Balkan air campaigns, Serbian forces knew they had to exert strict radar and firing discipline to reduce American and allied anti-SAM successes. This strict discipline proved to be a thorn in the side of allied air planners and pilots throughout the campaign.

How successful were the strikes on the first night? It certainly did not seem to be the knockout blow that occurred on the first night of attacks during *Desert Storm* in 1991, nor was it as spectacular as the strikes against Bagdad in 2003. Several contextual elements worked against NATO and in favor of Milosevic. First, although not a counteroffensive plan, Serbian forces did have a plan: disperse and survive. This allowed for their communications and control apparatus to remain relatively intact after the first wave of attacks. Second, almost all of the dispersed missile battalions and their deadly surface-to-air missiles remained intact as well as their acquisitions and fire control radars. NATO easily wrested control of the air from the RV I PVO, but it certainly did not gain air dominance after the first night. Most importantly, Milosevic did not capitulate. Twenty-four hours into the campaign, Serbian military forces, with the exception of the Yugoslav Air Force, still had the ability to resist NATO attacks.

Still, NATO severely damaged the RV I PVO's ability to wage war. The first night, NATO aircraft, USAF, and RNLAF shot down three MiG-29s. The Yugoslav forces inadvertently shot down one of their MiG-29s in a friendly fire incident. The RV I PVO's total number of MiG-29s decreased from 16 to 12. Exact figures are difficult to ascertain, but the first night's attacks damaged or destroyed at least a dozen MiG-21s, and the Serbian hopes that aircraft moved into hardened aircraft shelters had a good chance of surviving proved absolute folly, as allied munitions sliced through their reinforced concrete roofs and obliterated the aircraft parked inside. Of the Yugoslav Air Force's 44 MiG-21s, perhaps two dozen survived the opening salvo of the war. In all probability, of those aircraft that survived from both the MiG-29s and MiG-21s, it is doubtful that even half of those were airworthy.

While Serbian forces did not attack NATO forces in neighboring countries, they did begin air attacks against elements of the Kosovo Liberation Army. J-22 Oraos of the 98th Fighter Bomber Regiment (241st and 252nd Squadrons) and G-4 Super Galebs from the 229th Squadron dropped BL755 cluster bombs and FAB-250 Soviet-designed general-purpose bombs on known KLA positions. On one of the first strikes, KLA forces successfully brought down one of the J-22s. These were dangerous missions for the Yugoslav pilots. NATO air power ensured that any Yugoslav Air Force aircraft had to fly at extremely low levels, hit their targets, and return to base, all the while hoping that any NATO fighters flying combat air patrols overhead did not discover them.

Night two

NATO did not wait another 24 hours before resuming the attacks, although unlike *Desert Storm*, attacks did occur "around the clock." Serbian forces spent the day of the 25th collecting their breath and continuing their dispersal efforts. Aircraft from the 251st Fighter-Bomber Squadron moved some aircraft, and helicopters departed Batajnica. Prior to the second night of air attacks, Secretary General Javier Solana and SACEUR, Gen Wesley Clark, held a press

Although a more recent shot, this photo shows two of the Serbian Air Force's MiG-29s. The RV I PVO's fleet of MiG-29s was decimated when they launched to defend their air space. (Srdan Popović/CC-BY-SA-4.0)

OPPOSITE TARGETS HIT IN DOWNTOWN BELGRADE

briefing. That afternoon before the second day of attacks began Gen Clark stated, "We are going to systematically and progressively attack, disrupt, degrade, devastate and ultimately destroy these forces and their facilities and support, unless President Milosevic complies with the demands of the international community. In that respect the operation will be as long and difficult as President Milosevic requires it to be." NATO aircraft returned to the skies in the late afternoon.

At around 1630hrs on Thursday May 25, the next wave of attacks began. On the second night only 64 aircraft participated in strikes, a harbinger that weather was going to be a significant hindrance to ongoing operations. NATO forces again hit airfields and barracks of air defense personnel. The second night of air attacks by NATO aircrews also demonstrated a gradual escalation, with increased and heavier attacks. Targets included the Armed Forces of Serbia and Montenegro (VJ) barracks at Urosevac and Prizren in Kosovo; the military airfields at Nis in southern Serbia and Golubovci near Podgorica, Montenegro; and other Serb military facilities near Trstenik and Danilovgrad. Only about ten SAMs were fired the second night with no allied losses. This might have lulled NATO air planners into a false sense of security.

More B-52Hs took off from RAF Fairford, but after expending their munitions, their return flight took them back to Barksdale Air Force Base. Other B-52Hs, having previously departed from Barksdale, then landed fully armed and ready for the next mission. This was part of the rolling changeover program. B-52s conducted a mission and returned to Barksdale, while the strike sorties flew from their home base to RAF Fairford. Other B-52s also arrived from Diego Garcia and Fairchild AFB.

Night three
On the eve of the third night of strikes, NATO had suffered no losses and only minimal interference from Serbian air defense forces. While this was certainly a positive sign, NATO leaders recognized that at this early stage in the operation, the bombing was having little to no visible effect. Air Commodore David J. G. Wilby, a NATO spokesperson, noted that thus far, "There is no evidence that ongoing Serb counter insurgency operations will cease. Fighting continues in the Northern and South-Western areas of Kosovo. In addition there is evidence of a build-up of armoured units in the border area…"

Night three of the air campaign, NATO expected to find the Serbian forces on their heels, ready to surrender, and provide the NATO air campaign planners with a suitable off-ramp

A B-52H Stratofortress taxis to a ramp after a mission at RAF Fairford, United Kingdom. (USAF)

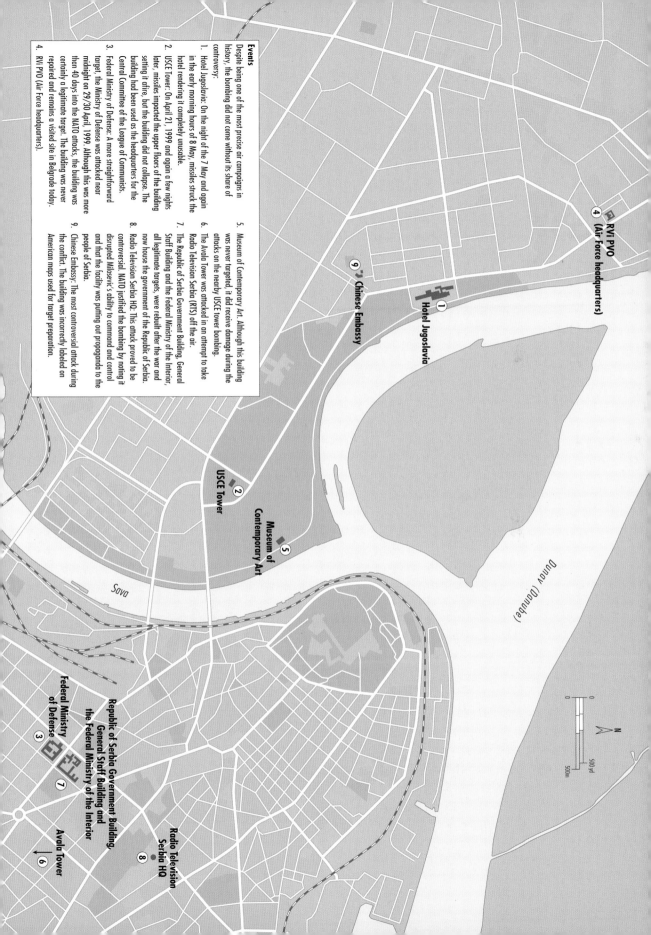

Events

Despite being one of the most precise air campaigns in history, the bombing did not come without its share of controversy:

1. Hotel Jugoslavia: On the night of the 7 May and again in the early morning hours of 8 May, missiles struck the hotel rendering it completely unusable.

2. USCE Tower: On April 21, 1999 and again a few nights later, missiles impacted the upper floors of the building setting it afire, but the building did not collapse. The building had been used as the headquarters for the Central Committee of the League of Communists.

3. Federal Ministry of Defense: A more straightforward target, the Ministry of Defense was attacked near midnight on 29/30 April, 1999. Although this was more than 40 days into the NATO attack, the building was certainly a legitimate target. The building was never repaired and remains a visited site in Belgrade today.

4. RVi PVO (Air Force headquarters).

5. Museum of Contemporary Art. Although this building was never targeted, it did receive damage during the attacks on the nearby USCE tower bombing.

6. The Avala Tower was attacked in an attempt to take Radio Television Serbia (RTS) off the air.

7. The Republic of Serbia Government Building, General Staff Building and the Federal Ministry of the Interior, all legitimate targets, were rebuilt after the war and now house the government of the Republic of Serbia.

8. Radio Television Serbia HQ: This attack proved to be controversial. NATO justified the bombing by noting it disrupted Milosevic's ability to command and control and that the facility was putting out propaganda to the people of Serbia.

9. Chinese Embassy: The most controversial attack during the conflict. The building was incorrectly labeled on American maps used for target preparation.

RVi PVO (Air Force headquarters)

"Chinese Embassy

Hotel Jugoslavia

USCE Tower

Museum of Contemporary Art

Sava

Dunav (Danube)

Federal Ministry of Defense

Republic of Serbia Government Building, General Staff Building and the Federal Ministry of the Interior

Radio Television Serbia HQ

Avala Tower

N

500m
500 yd

to ease up on their bombing efforts. Nothing was farther from the truth. One report noted that the gradually increasing pressure of the air campaign, similar to the Vietnam-era *Rolling Thunder*, was having no effect at all, stating it, "…merely allowed the Serbs to adjust to a new level of pain, while pressing ahead with what they had planned all along: to redouble their effort to run as many ethnic Albanian civilians as possible out of Kosovo and thus be able to take an unobstructed shot at the KLA once and for all."

Attacks on the third night increased in Kosovo, going from 20 percent the previous two nights to 40 percent on the third night, although weather over Belgrade played a role in the increased attacks. In response to a lack of movement on behalf of the Serbian military and police forces, General Clark met with Solana, and the UN Secretary General ordered an expansion of the air campaign and an increase in strikes. Third night attacks also closely approached the outskirts of Belgrade. Whether or not this was meant to send the message of a tightening noose around Milosevic's neck is conjecture, but for the time being the attacks seemed to be having little effect on his calculus. Night three saw 17 targets attacked in two waves.

Rather than the third night being NATO's denouement, the campaign entered a new phase, and that night proved exceptionally busy for NATO and Yugoslav forces. For NATO forces, one F-15C of the 493rd Fighter Squadron, the "Grim Reapers," destroyed two MiG-29s in the same engagement. On the other side, members of the 3rd Battery of the 250th Air Defense Missile Brigade, under the command of Colonel Zoltan Dani, brought down an F-117.

Shooting down of Vega-31

On the night of March 27, 1999, the weather heavily influenced operations. No EA-6B Prowlers took off, but a package of F-117s was already headed for its targets around Belgrade. One major mistake in this night's operations was that the F-117s entered the country flying

Munitions experts of the USAF prepare to load a laser-guided bomb into an F-117 stealth fighter. The nose art on the aircraft indicates this particular F-117 belongs to the 8th Fighter Squadron, the "Black Sheep." (Keith Reed/U.S. AIR FORCE/ AFP via Getty Images)

the exact flight path they had the previous two nights. Serbian observers had noted the take-off times of these aircraft and relayed that information back to Serbia, which then informed the SAM operators. The F-117s had flown similar flight paths the previous two nights, and on this night they flew without the support of the EA-6B's radar jamming capabilities. The 250th Air Defense Missile Brigade moved its SA-3 Goas (S-125 Neva/Pechora) into this flight path. This gave the commanders and officers of the SAM batteries a very good idea of precisely when the F-117s would be passing overhead. In addition, Serbian forces also knew that the EA-6Bs had not taken off that evening. This allowed Serbian air defense sites to radiate at will without fear of drawing one of the EA-6Bs' HARM missiles.

It is worth noting here that the F-117 Nighthawk is not an "invisible" aircraft to radar. Rather, it is known simply as "low observable." Low-observable aircraft are purpose built to reduce the aircraft's radar cross-section (RCS), making it significantly more difficult, but not impossible, for enemy air defenses to locate, track, and engage the aircraft. Numerous aspects of RCS reduction are taken into account to reduce the RCS, including "shaping" of the aircraft, radar-absorbent material (RAM), and disguising aircraft heat emissions. Another important aspect of the F-117 was that its only defense mechanism was its stealth characteristics. It has no radar warning, no chaff, and no flares. It predicated its entire defense on not being tracked by radar.

The 250th Air Defense Missile Brigade activated its P-18 very high frequency radar and began looking on its scopes for any incoming aircraft. According to some sources, they were able to pick up the F-117 approaching Serbia, as it turned left and right on its predetermined path (pilots of the F-117 and other American sources dispute this was a tactic). The commander of the SAM battery, Lieutenant Colonel Zoltan Dani, ordered his fire control radar (FCR) turned on. The FCR swept across the sky on three separate occasions, and just as the F-117 pilot Lieutenant Colonel Dale Zelko, call sign VEGA-31, opened his bomb bay doors to release his munitions, Colonel Dani's crew definitively picked up the F-117 and achieved a radar and missile lock.

Up in the cockpit, Zelko had just finished his bomb run over Belgrade in his F-117 (82-0806) when the improbable occurred. Off to his right, out the right window of his

The shooting-down of Vega-31

The low-observable F-117 Nighthawk stealth fighter was the pride of the United States Air Force's modern and highly technologically advanced fleet of aircraft. First used during the invasion of Panama in 1989, but to greater effect during Operation *Desert Storm*, the F-117 proved itself by flying into dangerous and heavily defended enemy territory and surviving. The aircraft was oddly shaped, multifaceted, and covered in nearly black radar-absorbent material (RAM). The shaping and coatings allowed radar waves to bounce off and away from the aircraft instead of back toward the ground. All of this rendered the F-117 very difficult to track and engage.

Lieutenant Colonel Dale Zelko, a veteran F-117 pilot from Operation *Desert Storm*, flew on the opening night of strikes for both *Desert Storm* and *Allied Force*. He was flying again on the evening of March 27, 1999, in aircraft 82-0806, and had just finished his bombing run near Belgrade, when the 250th Air Defense Missile battery stationed at Simanovci launched a pair of SA-3 missiles.

This particular F-117 had the nickname "Something Wicked" painted inside of the weapons bay doors, and the missiles from the 250th certainly indicated that "something wicked this way comes." The F-117 had just released two EGBU-27 against the Strazevica command center. During his bomb run, the radar operators below used their P-18 radar to track Zelko's F-117. It is possible that Serbian radar received a solid radar return when the F-117's weapons bay doors were open.

Lt Col Zelko watched the two S-125 Neva (SA-3 GOA) missiles as they arched over and headed directly for his aircraft. He later remembered, "You know what? This is bad. I don't think I'm going to skinny through this one." He was right. The first missile passed above the F-117 but did not proximity fuse, and this might have saved Zelko's life. The second missile continued on its flight path directly at the F-117. Zelko had enough time to think, "It's going to run right into me." The missile impacted or exploded directly under the left wing of the F-117 and sent it into a violent uncontrolled spin. The Serbian IADS operators had done the impossible: shot down a stealth fighter.

MH-60G Pave Hawks were important CSAR assets. An HH-60G like the one seen here rescued Lt Col Dale Zelko after his F-117 was shot down. (USAF)

canopy, Zelko caught sight of two bright lights as two SA-3 missiles lifted off. The first missile passed close enough for Zelko to feel the aircraft shaking, but the missile's proximity fuse did not ignite. Zelko focused on the second missile and had just enough time to think, "It's going to run right into me." The second missile exploded on contact with the F-117's left wing. The Serbians did what Iraq could not during *Desert Storm*; they had shot down the vaunted "stealth fighter." As the missile detonated, the aircraft went into a violent negative-G roll. Zelko later noted he was in severe negative-Gs as he was being pulled from his seat, toward his canopy, and away from his ejection handles. Zelko, now in a violently spinning aircraft that was disintegrating around him, reached down and pulled the ejection handles.

As Zelko floated down under his parachute canopy, he carried with him standard survival equipment including a radio, first aid and medical packs, and other items a pilot would need once on the ground. In his flight suit tucked under one arm he also carried a carefully folded American flag from one of his squadron's intelligence airmen – the same senior airman who had aided in the preparation of his target package for that night's strike. A longstanding tradition in the USAF had pilots and aircrews carry American flags with them during missions to hand out or gift as mementoes. Another F-117 pilot engaged in combat operations with Zelko was Major Elwood Hinman, also a member of the 8th Fighter Squadron. Hinman stated years after the war that "if we had to pick one man we wanted to be in that situation, it would have been Zelko." Zelko, as the 49th Fighter Wing's life support officer, was the officer charged with training other F-117 pilots in the instruction of ejection procedures, survival equipment, and the steps to take should they find themselves in enemy territory.

Almost immediately after ejecting from his stricken fighter, Zelko found himself floating serenely under his parachute canopy and descending toward Serbia. Realizing that his rescue radio had more of a chance of sending distress calls while he was relatively in the "line of sight" of other airborne assets, he made the unusual decision to make a radio call while still floating to earth. Zelko called: "Mayday. Mayday. Mayday, Vega-31." Orbiting in nearby safe air space, a NATO airborne warning and control system aircraft did pick up his transmission. A controller in the back of the E-3 responded with: "Magic-86, on guard, go ahead."

The E-3 was not the only aircraft that heard Zelko's next words, and blood ran cold from the skies over Serbia all the way back to the CAOC: "Roger, Vega-31 is out of the aircraft! Downed." A nearby F-117, Vega-32, captured the entire event on an internal cockpit recorder and can be heard to say, "Oh damn" and exhale audibly. Zelko then turned on his extremely shrill locator beacon. As soon as Zelko turned on the beacon, the AWACS attempted to contact him again. Between the beacon and Magic-86's communication attempt, neither party heard the other.

Zelko was using a short-range rescue radio intended only for communicating with aircraft orbiting overhead as part of a search and rescue attempt, which meant that he had difficulty in coordinating directly with the airborne warning and control system aircraft. Luckily, another aircraft stepped in. A KC-135 refueler orbiting in its predetermined orbit over Bosnia and Herzegovina started relaying messages from Zelko to the NATO E-3. The KC-135 call sign "Frank-36" began trying to relay Zelko's distress call to the E-3, telling the AWACS "…it sounds like he got out of the aircraft." In all probability, the go-between on Frank-36 did not know who or what Vega-31 was. Vega-32 was the only aircraft that seemed to be hearing all of the communications between Zelko, the KC-135, and the NATO E-3 AWACS. Other F-117s now broke radio silence and tried to contact Zelko directly but received no response. Vega-11 called Zelko, and Vega-21 called that "Vega-31 ejected." Meanwhile, 450 miles away, the approach controller at Aviano Air Base also tried to contact Vega-31 who, by this point, was rapidly approaching the ground outside Belgrade. Zelko later joked, "I was not ready to land."

For nearly two minutes, no one had heard from Vega-31, but then he popped up on the radio again. At the same time, Vega-21 called to "start the CSAR effort." Back in the CAOC an officer who was working on the combat operations floor that night said, "You could have heard a pin drop when we realized it was a stealth." Then, almost instantaneously after the flash of dumbfounded silence, all hell broke loose. An American F-117 pilot was on the ground in enemy territory. He needed to be found, pinpointed, positively identified, and rescued before Serbian forces could capture him. The enemy forces were closer and already had a head start.

For over five minutes, Lieutenant Colonel Dale Zelko continued to call mayday into his rescue radio before he finally landed roughly five miles west of Belgrade. He was just south of the nearest town of Ruma. With his location so close to the capital city and inside a heavily defended air space, combat search and rescue officers recognized this was going to be a very difficult mission.

Zelko's peaceful reverie and float down to the ground came to an abrupt end as he landed in a flat field. His first order of business after freeing himself from his parachute was to bury and conceal what he could and then find somewhere suitable to camouflage himself.

Although often overlooked, the U.S. Navy and Marine Corps EA-6Bs played an important role in suppression of enemy air defense and provided electronic countermeasures and jamming for NATO strike packages on a nightly basis. Their absence on the third night of attacks proved disastrous when NATO lost an F-117 to an SA-3. (USAF/Getty Images)

A U.S. Air Force Kc-135 takes off on a refueling mission on March 26, 1999, for Nato Operation *Allied Force*. (U.S. Air Force (USAF/Getty Images)

Meanwhile, overhead, F-16CJs began "chainsawing" back and forth close to Zelko's position and a tanker in order to be on scene for the rescue effort they knew was getting under way. Even at this moment, aircrews dropped their current mission and turned their attention to the rescue of the downed aviator. Vega-32 also radioed back to Magic and gave the closest approximate location to where Zelko had ejected.

Zelko landed roughly two miles from the wreckage of his aircraft. The F-117 impacted upside down and on fire, creating a beacon for anyone nearby. This also meant that Zelko was extremely close to the Serbian forces who began searching for him. The JNA knew it would be a great propaganda victory should they capture the F-117 pilot and knew they needed to find him before the American combat search and rescue team arrived. Zelko set off from his landing site, moving away from the wreck of the F-117. He needed to put distance between himself, his landing site, and the downed aircraft, where the Serbians would begin their search for him. Zelko crawled into an irrigation ditch and moved away from his impact point, seeking somewhere to conceal himself and await rescue.

As Zelko waited and hoped, dozens of aircraft began a pre-coordinated ballet necessary to place the rescue force directly over Zelko's hiding spot. CSAR forces trained relentlessly for moments like these, but the rescue effort was so much larger than just the rescue helicopters. That night, more than a dozen airborne assets were immediately re-tasked to participate in the rescue. These assets included at least two airborne warning and control system aircraft (NATO and Air Force); three intelligence, surveillance, and reconnaissance assets; an RC-135 Rivet Joint and an RC-135 Compass Call; a U-2; and an EC-130E airborne command and control center. In addition, four F-16 CJs, which provided on-scene command until the arrival of the A-10s, and USMC EA-6Bs finally took to the sky that night. Each provided unique capabilities to the rescue of one downed individual. Furthermore, because of national and NATO training exercises, aircrews were prepared to launch into a rescue mission upon a moment's notice. Since all pilots prepared and trained to be shot down and then evade the enemy, and because every pilot that night knew exactly their role in the rescue effort, NATO forces had a huge advantage over the Serbian forces who were looking for Zelko.

Weather had severely limited the number of strike aircraft flying on this third night, and this might have proven advantageous for the rescue forces and for those who initially heard Zelko's mayday cry. Luckily, there were fewer aircraft in the air, and thus, this limited what could have turned into a communication crisis with too many voices clogging the airwaves. Once it became apparent an American airman had been shot down, all other missions ceased. The KC-135 refuelers, which normally flew in preplanned orbits far outside of any enemy threat ring, pushed dangerously closer to Serbia. This move put them closer to enemy MiGs and surface-to-air missile systems.

An important aspect of the rescue effort was the need for the incoming CSAR members to definitively identify and authenticate the downed pilot. This was done using the isolated personnel report (ISOPREP) information. Each member of an American aircrew filled out a sheet that was then kept in their unit and immediately forwarded to rescue personnel in the event of a shoot-down such as this. Each ISOPREP form contained information that only the downed person would know. Other members of the on-scene rescue leads in the A-10s had raced to the 8th Fighter Squadron to obtain Zelko's ISOPREP information and then relayed it to the A-10 pilots providing on-scene command.

The A-10 pilots in contact with Zelko on the ground asked the downed flier, a self-proclaimed numismatist, what his favorite coin was. Zelko responded with the "Mercury dime." This correct answer was clearly not something the enemy forces could guess or force

Propaganda leaflet following the shoot-down of F-117. Note that the leaflet incorrectly attributes three F-117 losses to the RV I PVO defence forces. (Clay Gilliland/CC-SA-2.0)

An EA-6B HARM shot

The EA-6B Prowler remains one of the unsung heroes of the conflicts of the 1990s. The EA-6B was the only U.S. airborne radar-jamming system available to protect U.S. Navy, Marine Corps, Air Force, and coalition aircraft, and it was the only aircraft that flew with every single strike mission in the Balkans.

The EA-6B was a four-person variant of the U.S. Navy's A-6 Intruder. The four crew members included a pilot and three other naval flight officers (NFOs) who worked onboard as electronic warfare officers (EWO) or electronic countermeasures officers (ECMO).

During *Allied Force*, Prowlers typically flew their missions carrying two AN/ALQ-99 electronic jamming devices under the wings and two or three external fuel tanks, plus one AGM-55 HARM. The extra fuel allowed the Prowlers to remain on-station for five hours or more, providing ECM support to other strike aircraft. EA-6Bs operating from the USS *Roosevelt* found themselves operating closer to Serbia and Kosovo than the land-launched EA-6Bs flying out of Aviano. This allowed the carrier Prowlers to fly with a single fuel tank, so one more of the underwing pylons was available for an additional AGM-88 HARM.

EA-6Bs flew in a "race track" pattern in pairs orbiting at 15,000ft within range of surface-to-air missiles, but above AAA fire. The Prowlers flew in such a way that while the first aircraft was in a turn or in its outbound lag from the target position, the other was flying inbound to the objective, in order to continuously blind the enemy radars. This kept a constant stream of radar-jamming pointing at the enemy radars, even if the effectiveness of one of the emitters was reduced by the fact that an aircraft was turning.

Remnants of Lt. Col Dale Zelko's F-117, including the canopy, ejection seat, and a section of the wing, now sit in the Museum of Aviation in Belgrade. (Andrej Isakovic/AFP via Getty Images)

out of Zelko if he had been captured, and they were setting an aerial ambush for the CSAR forces. The on-scene A-10s authenticated Zelko and the rescue helicopters proceeded in for the final and most harrowing part of the rescue.

The rescue force itself consisted of two MH-53 Pave Lows and one MH-60 Pave Hawk. Flying just above the treetops, the pilot of one of the rescue helicopters called, "two miles out." At that same moment, Serbian surface-to-air radars began transmitting and targeting the A-10s. As their radar homing and warning sounds began emitting in their headsets, one of the A-10 pilots made an unusual radio call. Transmitting into the open, he called "Magnum." Magnum was the code word used by the F-16CJ pilots to denote the firing of a HARM anti-radar missile at the radar emitters of the Serbians. The A-10 pilot figured, if the Serbian air defense forces had the ability to listen in, then maybe they would hear the Magnum call and turn off their radars. Almost as soon as the pilot made the false call, the Serbians turned off their radars. Whether the Serbians actually turned off their radars as part of emission control or as a direct result of the false radio call is irrelevant; the A-10s were free to focus on the effort at hand.

The three helicopters thundered in low overhead of Zelko's position. The MH-60 located the survivor and moved overhead, and the two MH-53s circled overhead in a Lufbery circle, each one covering a 180-degree arc around the actual rescue helicopter. Above them, the A-10s did the same and ensured complete 360-degree coverage over the pilot. The MH-60 Pave Hawk, call sign Gator-31, settled onto the ground and a pararescueman jumped out for the final authentication. A mere 40 seconds later, Zelko was inside the helicopter and the entire mission began the race out of enemy air space.

Another F-117 pilot noted that back at Aviano, the F-117 prepared a short-notice strike to drop LGBs on the wreckage of Zelko's downed aircraft in an effort to destroy any sensitive materials or stymie collection efforts, but locals and news crews from Serbia arrived before that strike could be carried out. By the next morning, the F-117 wreckage appeared on news outlets across the globe. The canopy with the name "Capt Ken 'Wiz' Dwelle" drew particular attention, and reporters rushed to his home of record in Alamogordo, New Mexico, the home of the F-117s. The news crews were unaware that the name on the side of the aircraft had nothing to do with which pilot was actually in the cockpit for any given mission; they were surprised when Captain Dwelle – who was not deployed – answered the door and informed the news crews, "I reported that plane stolen months ago!" Much of the downed F-117 ended up on display at the Museum of Aviation, Belgrade, Serbia, including the shattered canopy, ejection seat, and an entire wing.

Later reports indicated that another F-117, tail number 837, also received serious damage from a SAM, but was able to return to base. The USAF has never admitted to this later incident, although a website dedicated to the memory of the F-117s lists this jet as having suffered damage in May of 1999.

A double MiG kill

Also on March 26, Captain Jeffery Hwang of the 493rd Fighter Squadron shot down a pair of MiG-29s. This particular dogfight proved a bit problematic. Not only was Captain Hwang's radio only intermittently transmitting, but because of this communication issue, Captain Hwang and his wingman, "Boomer" McMurry, were both firing missiles without de-conflicting their targets, so McMurry and Hwang both fired AIM-120s at the lead MiG. Hwang then fired a second AIM-120 at the MiG-29 in trail. Although there was considerable confusion about whose missile hit the lead MiG, it was later determined that Hwang's missiles had shot down both MiG-29s, making him the first American F-15 pilot to score a double MiG kill in the same engagement. The same F-15C Hwang flew that night (86-0156) remained in service with the USAF and the Air National Guard until April 2023, when it was decommissioned and flown for the final time to Dayton, Ohio, to join the National Museum of the United States Air Force.

The pilots of the MiG-29s were Major Slobodan Peric (aircraft 18114) and Captain 1st Class Zoran Radosavljevic. Peric ejected from his stricken MiG-29, but Radosavljevic did not escape the AIM-120 that hit his aircraft. Again, both MiG-29s suffered avionics and radar malfunctions, indicating that even when airworthy, the modern MiG-29s were no match for the NATO fighters. One book about the air war noted that Major Peric later argued with the RV I PVO commander, General Spasoje Smiljanic, telling the general that the MiG-29 pilots were being forced into combat with non-functioning aircraft. Supposedly, General Smiljanic responded, "All of you just want higher ranks! But you are not willing to die!" Ironically, Smiljanic later authored a book titled *NATO Aggression – Air Force and Air Defense in Defense of the Fatherland*.

SEAD campaign

Following the third night of attacks, NATO Spokesman Jaime Shea stated, "NATO's air operations are a last resort. This is not a trigger-happy organization. We have taken a long time to come to this painful decision to strike," but NATO, now three days into the campaign, needed to expand the air war. Two factors played a role in this expansion. First, the loss of the vaunted F-117 Nighthawk forced NATO planners to grapple directly with Serbian air defenses. Between March 31 and April 9, NATO launched an all-out campaign to suppress Serbian air defenses. Perhaps NATO and the United States in particular had not given enough credit to the air defense missile operators.

The second reason was the aforementioned use of Serbian air power against targets in Kosovo. NATO AWACS and members in the CAOC observed the RV I PVO's Super Galeb operations on day two and three of the

A Spanish Air Force EF-18A Hornet moves into position behind an Air Combat Command KC-135R Stratotanker of the 22nd Air Refueling Squadron during Operation *Allied Force*. (DOD)

campaign. The RV I PVO aircraft attacked both ethnic Albanian sites as well as the forces of the KLA.

Throughout *Allied Force*, the Serbians fired nearly as many surface-to-air missiles as Iraq did in 1991. On the one hand, allied aircrews in *Desert Storm* faced more missiles in a shorter amount of time, but over Serbia, allied aircrews were three times as likely to have a missile fired at them. Despite the case of the shoot-down of the F-117 on the third night of operations, Serbian IADS were not as successful as the Iraqis were during *Desert Storm*.

Since survival was the name of the game, Serbian SAM launches were more often against targets of opportunity than as part of a larger defensive effort. NATO aircrews also chose to fly at higher altitudes than Serbia's AAA and man-portable air defense systems (MANPADS) were capable of reaching. NATO used EA-6Bs, F-16CJs, and EC-130H to provide electronic jamming and suppression to nightly sorties. Of particular importance were the U.S. Navy EA-6Bs, capable of electronic warfare and attack. NATO attackers used both active jamming of Serbian systems and the kinetic launch of HARMs from a variety of aircraft to suppress the threat of the Serbian IADS.

However, by early April, the SEAD campaign bore fruit. NATO press representatives noted that active radar levels operating inside Serbia decreased noticeably. This allowed NATO aircraft the ability to loiter over Serbia more and hit more targets, and thus put even greater pressure on Milosevic. On March 31, Yugoslav forces lost a surveillance radar of the 230th Missile Regiment. It was the recipient of a HARM. The same day the 52nd Artillery Missile Air Defense Brigade lost its P-15 radar. Between April 4 and 9, Serbia continued to lose more radars and men. This started a slippery slope in which radars continued to be destroyed and NATO flew more sorties and destroyed more radars. As the IADS slowly broke down and the weather improved, NATO attacks across the country continued to increase. It now seemed that, as NATO was able to place more "shooters" in the sky, the time between when a radar began emitting and when a NATO aircraft fired a missile decreased significantly. Serbian forces slowly but surely began to lose their radar coverage and their ability to track NATO aircraft. Although Serbia had always planned to fight a defensive war, its ability to provide meaningful air defense was slowly eroding.

In this particular portion of the operation, both sides could take pride in their accomplishments. The Serbians did what the Iraqis could not – shoot down an F-117 – but the allies could point to only two crewed aircraft losses throughout the conflict. NATO

Although NATO might have held a technological edge during the campaign, Serbian forces used low-tech camouflage and concealment techniques to great advantage. Difficult to pick out even from this vantage point – and impossible from the air – a Serbian AAA piece sits well concealed. (Jack Guez/AFP via Getty Images)

The number one reason for NATO intervention in Serbia and Kosovo was to put an end to the ethnic cleansing of Kosovar Albanians. Here a member, not of the Yugoslav military, but a Serbian police officer, sits atop an armored personnel carrier during earlier cleansing operations in 1998. (Srdjan Suki/AFP via Getty Images)

could not render the IADS system ineffective, but the Serbians had relatively little success in shooting down NATO aircraft, considering the large numbers invading their air space every night. Despite the ever-present possibility of an active Serbian surface-to-air threat, NATO operations continued to increase unabated throughout the war. In the first few nights of the war, NATO averaged around 200 sorties. By the end of the conflict, over 1,000 sorties a day took to the skies. Even when one considers all of the other factors that eventually forced Milosevic to capitulate, the ever-increasing number of sorties being flown against his forces with no sign of abatement certainly influenced his thinking.

Ethnic cleansing increases

March 26 also saw an increase in Milosevic's desire to cleanse Kosovo of its entire ethnic Albanian population. That day, in the town of Suva Reka, Serbian police officers locked 50 members of one household into a pizzeria before throwing in grenades and shooting any survivors. Forty-eight people died, including women and children. Serbian police forces loaded the bodies in trucks, drove them to the vicinity of Belgrade, and placed them in a mass grave. Serbian forces specifically targeted individuals and families with links to the KLA or who had provided support to the OSCE mission.

NATO representative Air Commodore Wilby also noted, "Helicopters are being used against the civil population. Paramilitaries enter towns and villages and terrify the people; they are followed by the FRY military and police who give an official slant to these activities and cynically issue leaflets stating that now it is safe to leave the town or village." Of course, it was not safe for any ethnic Albanian to leave a city. The ethnic Albanian population found themselves caught in a catch-22. Stay where they were and await the arrival of Serbian forces who would, at best, force them to leave their homes, or attempt to flee on their own where they might run into Serbian forces and simply disappear forever.

Serbian atrocities and ethnic cleansing efforts forced NATO and the United Nations into dealing with a full-blown humanitarian crisis outside the borders of Serbia and Kosovo. Those forced from their homes or those who fled willingly flowed into neighboring countries. A NATO spokesman noted, "We are urgently formulating the organization and plans to dovetail the flow of aircraft carrying humanitarian aid in with the activities associated with our operational mission."

At another press conference, NATO officials made it clear that what was occurring in Kosovo followed a "prearranged pattern," indicating this was a long-planned-for event. In

Well before the opening salvoes of the conflict in March 1999, numerous countries attempted to deliver humanitarian aid to the Kosovo refugees. Here an unknown aircraft lands at Pristina in Kosovo. (SASA STANKOVIC/AFP via Getty Images)

Well before the opening salvoes of the conflict in March 1999, numerous countries attempted to deliver humanitarian aid to the Kosovo refugees. Here an unknown aircraft lands at Pristina in Kosovo. (SASA STANKOVIC/AFP via Getty Images)

other words, this was not a "knee-jerk" reaction or an ad hoc event but a well-orchestrated and thought-out event months in the making: "It represents a master plan that was conceived and well on its way to being executed before the first NATO bomb was dropped against a military target."

On the last day of March 1999, Kenneth Bacon, the U.S. Assistant Secretary of Defense for Public Affairs (ASD/PA) stepped up to a microphone in the briefing room at the Pentagon. As of this date, the air campaign was exactly one week old. Bacon mentioned that the headquarters of the Special Unit Corps of Serbia was the target of the previous night's strikes. The SUC was equivalent to Special Forces in other nations. Other targets included fielded forces operating in Kosovo, including tanks and APCs. However, in what would continue to be a significant problem hindering operations, ASD Bacon noted that it was increasingly difficult to conduct battle damage assessment and to obtain post-strike images since the weather was "quite bad including very low ceilings and clouds." Although not notable at the time, the daily briefings were similar to those held during Operation *Desert Storm*, but they were held even more often and demonstrated an almost constant source of information, photographs, and imagery from the ongoing campaign. While one might quibble as to whether or not *Allied Force* was the most precise air campaign in history, the media certainly covered it most heavily. The DOD and the U.S. Air Force in particular seemed only too happy to provide this material to a very willing media at the dawn of the 24-hour news cycle.

By early April, the humanitarian crisis continued to worsen, with 300,000 people having been forced from their homes in Kosovo and an additional 300,000 on the roads leading out of Kosovo. As NATO spokesperson Jamie Shea noted, "In fact if you wanted to do a 'back of the envelope' mathematical calculation, at this rate the Serb security forces would have more or less emptied Kosovo in between 10 to 20 days from now." The refugees flowed into Montenegro, Macedonia, and Albania, and the United Nations struggled to provide support to these countries and to the refugees themselves. The United Nations High Commissioner for Refugees (UNHCR) worked in conjunction with representatives from NATO to provide support. This included everything from meals ready to eat (MREs) to blankets, water, medicine, and other lifesaving and life-sustaining material and equipment.

General Sir Michael Jackson, Commander of the Allied Forces in the former Yugoslav Republic of Macedonia, directed relief operations and oversaw the construction of the blossoming refugee camps and the massive airlift supporting humanitarian operations. NATO member countries including Germany, Greece, Norway, Turkey, Canada, and the U.S. all agreed to accept refugees into their borders.

The air war drags on, but the weather improves

Rather than demonstrate resolve or force Milosevic to halt his ethnic cleansing, the gradual escalation of the air campaign allowed time for Yugoslav forces on the ground to increase their campaign of forcing the ethnic Albanians out of Kosovo, launching even greater atrocities, and attacking the KLA forces on the ground. One study noted that the first three days of the air campaign had "no sought-after effect on Serb behaviour whatsoever."

Thus, rather than a short and decisive campaign, NATO forces were at a roadblock, with Milosevic refusing to be cowed. General Wesley Clark, recognizing the air campaign was not achieving the desired results, gained approval from the NAC to move forward with phase two of the campaign. When phase one strikes failed to force a change in Milosevic's behavior or stem human rights violations, NATO attacks began occurring south of the 44th parallel, striking Milosevic's forces in Kosovo. On April 3, the campaign moved into phase 3, which included targets in and around the city center of Belgrade. Again, the changes in phases did not occur because NATO met certain goals or criteria, but rather because the attacks were not having the desired effects.

As previously, mentioned, the first campaign objective was to roll back the Serbian IADS system and to destroy as many fire control radar and SAM sites as possible as part of the early SEAD campaign. This proved considerably more difficult than it had during Operation *Desert Storm*. Serbian forces proved extremely adept at emissions control or limiting the time their FCRs transmitted, making it difficult to achieve a lock and to fire a HARM missile at it. Serbian forces dispersed their SAM sites and radar sites before the war. Where they had the ability, the RV I PVO moved the SAM sites throughout the campaign. Using both emission control and dispersal tactics meant that rather than successfully rolling back the IADS, allied aircrews had to contend with enemy SAM activity throughout the campaign.

Two weeks into the air campaign General Wesley Clark, SACEUR, briefs United States Secretary of Defense William S. Cohen. Clark pleaded with Cohen to deliver him more combat aircraft for the operation. (NATO/ Getty Images)

Two B-1B "Bones" sit on the airfield at RAF Fairford. Although showing up after the start of hostilities, the B-1s provided an important all-weather capability. (USAF)

The Serb forces proved they were not simply going to be compliant targets and await NATO missiles to rain down on them.

At the same time that NATO sought to silence the air defense system, attacks increased against Serbian fielded forces, including military, paramilitary, police, and the Ministry of Internal Affairs (MUP) forces in Kosovo. It was clear as the first week of the campaign came to a close that Milosevic was operating in a "siege mentality."

As the campaign entered April, NATO brought other aircraft to bear against Serbian forces. At RAF Fairford, B-1B Lancers from the 77th Bomb Squadron of the 28th Bomb Wing arrived from Ellsworth Air Force Base, South Dakota. The B-1B Lancer, more commonly known as the B-1 Bone, had an important all-weather capability. To keep the ever-growing armada in the air, the U.S. brought in more KC-135 tankers. Still, weather and the Serbian forces refused to cooperate with NATO goals. Serbian forces in the southern portion of the country used dispersal and concealment tactics to frustrate NATO attacks. More than half of NATO strike aircraft returned to their bases with ordnance still hanging on their wings.

One thing that did go NATO's way was the cessation of attacks against Kosovar forces by the J-22s and the G-4s of the RV I PVO. NATO obviously knew the local forces were under air strikes from the Yugoslav aircraft and stepped up attacks against air bases and aircraft parked on the tarmac. No Yugoslav Air Force aircraft attacked Kosovar forces after April 4.

By April 5, NATO attacks could best be described as "more." On this date more bridges, air defense radars and communication sites, airfields, police headquarters, and petroleum facilities found themselves the recipients of increasing attacks. Although some media outlets begin to feel the war was dragging on, with improved weather came more and improved attacks. There was, however, a growing sense of desperation about the fielded forces operating along the border and inside Kosovo as stated at a NATO briefing: "we have not achieved the level of damage on these forces that we would have liked."

On April 6, the United States Secretary of Defense William Cohen arrived at NATO headquarters. Other NATO foreign ministers seeking an end to the air campaign, but more importantly to the humanitarian crisis, followed him. The same day that Secretary Cohen arrived, the Federal Republic of Yugoslavia offered a unilateral ceasefire, but provided no further concessions or any indications the country was willing to comply with

Seen here is a Panavia Tornado from the JbG-32 (Fighter-Bomber Wing) of the German Air Force stationed at Lechfeld, Germany. This Tornado has just received a top off of gas from an American KC-135R Stratotanker. Note that the Tornado is carrying AIM-9 sidewinders and an AGM-88 HARM. (USAF)

NATO demands. NATO leaders judged this pledge insufficient. NATO spokesperson Jamie Shea noted:

> A cease-fire is of course necessary, but it is not sufficient, it cannot simply wipe the slate clean and take us back to the status quo ante, particularly as a cease-fire says nothing about the actions of those paramilitary units in Kosovo that we believe are directly responsible at the moment for the systematic looting of homes and burning of homes and forced expulsion of Kosovo Albanian civilians towards the borders.

NATO leaders, including President Clinton of the United States, President Chirac of France, and Chancellor Schröder of Germany, all spoke out against Milosevic and noted that a ceasefire was not enough. President Clinton stated, "It is not enough for Milosevic to say that his forces will cease fire in Kosovo – he must withdraw his forces, let the refugees return safely to Kosovo, restore self-government for the Kosovars, and permit the deployment of an international security force." NATO Secretary General Javier Solana issued a statement saying, "The unilateral cease-fire proposed by Yugoslavia and the government of Serbia is clearly insufficient. Before a cease-fire can be considered, President Milosevic must meet the demands of the international community." Air attacks would continue until Milosevic indicated he was willing to comply with UN and NATO demands.

NATO's response to Milosevic posited that for the air campaign to end, Milosevic must first answer five questions:

> Is President Milosevic prepared for a verifiable cessation of all combat activities and killings? Is he prepared to withdraw military police and paramilitary forces from Kosovo? Is he prepared to agree to the deployment of an international security force? Is he prepared to permit the return of all refugees and unimpeded access for humanitarian aid? Is he prepared to put in place a political framework for Kosovo on the basis of the Rambouillet Accords?" [2]

2   Source: https://1997-2001.state.gov/briefings/statements/1999/ps990406.html

General Wesley K. Clark, the Supreme Allied Commander for Europe (SACEUR), points to targets inside Kosovo during a briefing held on April 13, 1999. It was near this time that Clark asked American and NATO leaders for more combat aircraft to continue the campaign. (HERWIG VERGULT/BELGA/AFP via Getty Images)

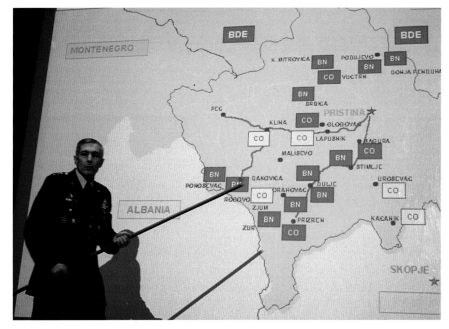

A new weapon of war emerges

One of the more interesting aspects of Operation *Allied Force* was the large-scale inclusion of unmanned aerial vehicles (UAVs) used by NATO forces during the conflict. Some noted that *Allied Force* was the first true "drone war." Although they have since become synonomous with modern warfare, their use during the Balkan campaigns was almost a novelty as the United States, Great Britain, and Germany began inserting UAVs into their existing tactics and techniques. A *New York Times* article noted, on May 3, that "light unmanned aerial vehicles known as drones are crisscrossing the skies over Kosovo, acting as electronic scouts, finding and filming elusive targets, especially Serbian troops hidden in bunkers or woods, and sending those images immediately to fighter jets overhead." NATO participants used their new UAVs extensively throughout the campaign to locate Serbian forces in Kosovo and relay that information back to both the CAOC and to fighters flying overhead. Thus, rather than flying traditional ISR missions, UAVs also acted as forward air controllers (FACs). UAVs could also conduct battle damage assessment rapidly in near-real time.

The RQ-1A Predator saw combat during the earlier Balkan conflict as part of Operation *Deny Flight*, although at the time the CIA still controlled the Predators. The USAF began full operational ownership of the new ISR platform during *Allied Force*. The USAF described the RQ-1 as an "un-armed, medium-altitude, long-endurance remotely piloted aircraft that is employed primarily as an intelligence-collection asset." Later versions used during the Afghanistan and Iraq conflicts would be armed, and the aircraft would drop the "R" reconnaissance designation for the "M" multi-role.

The United States also employed the IAI RQ-5 Hunter, a short-range UAV meant primarily for the U.S. Army and used at the division and corps levels. The RQ-5s were based out of Skopje International Airport in Macedonia as part of the U.S. Army's Task Force Hunter.

On April 7, a Hunter UAV was shot down by a Serbian Mi-8 Hip helicopter. In this engagement, the door gunner of the Mi-8 shot down the UAV. Between April 12 and 14, the German Luftwaffe lost three reconnaissance UAVs (CL-289 drones).

On April 18, the USAF admitted an RQ-1 had crashed as the result of a "combination of mechanical and human factors." According to the accident investigation board report (convened in the case of any lost aircraft including UAVs), the Predator experienced a fuel problem during its descent into Tuzla. The aircraft entered what the report called "meteorological conditions." These conditions were extremely cold temperatures inside a cloudbank that immediately caused aircraft icing. The RQ-1, now too heavy to maintain flight, lost engine power and its ability to stay airborne. The two Predator pilots, who controlled the aircraft from a ground station, executed critical action procedures but were unable to land the aircraft safely. It crashed in a wooded area four miles south of Tuzla.

Other UAV losses during the campaign included the American Predator UAV, serial number AF 95 021) from the 57th Wing at Nellis Air Force Base, Nevada, which crashed in the village of Talinovci, near the Pristina–Urosevac road at around 1645hrs on May 20. The remains of this Predator made an appealing moral victory for Serbian forces, and the wreckage was displayed on Serbian TV. This particular incident was the second Predator shot down in less than a week.

During the entirety of Operation *Allied Force* the United States lost 17 UAVs (three Predators, nine Hunters, four Pioneers, and one UAV of undetermined type), the German Luftwaffe lost seven (all of them the CL-289 turbojet drones), the French Air Force lost five (three Crécerelle, two CL-289) and the Royal Air Force lost 14 (all 14 Phoenix). Since downed aircraft in large conflicts can sometimes be difficult to account for, especially unmanned aircraft, there were another four UAVs lost of undetermined origin (possibly U.S., German, or Italian).

Naval aviation joins the attack

The aircraft carrier USS *Theodore Roosevelt* had departed Norfolk Navy Base on March 26 and was steaming toward the Persian Gulf to relieve the USS *Enterprise* and conduct operations in support of the ongoing Operation *Southern Watch* when it received orders to sail to the Ionian Sea to join the attacks of *Allied Force*. The U.S. Navy joined the fray on the night of April 6 and the early morning hours of the 7th as elements from Carrier Air Wing Eight aboard the USS *Theodore Roosevelt* prepared for action. This included F-14As from VF-41 "Black Aces" and VF-14 Tophatters, FA-18s of VFA-15 Valions and VFA-87 Golden Warriors, and WA-6B Prowlers from the VAQ-141 Shadowhawks providing

Arriving roughly a week after the start of hostilities, the aircraft carrier USS *Theodore Roosevelt* brought Carrier Air Wing Eight to the fight. (U.S. Navy/Getty Images)

On board the USS *Theodore Roosevelt*, aviation ordnancemen load Rockeye cluster bombs onto an aircraft's pylons. (U.S. Navy)

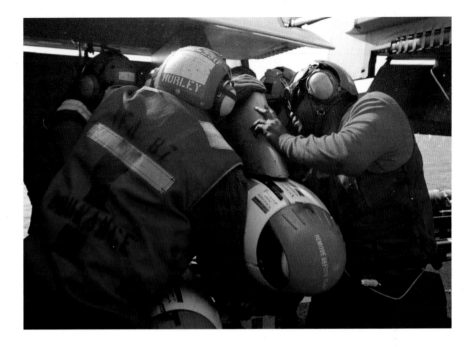

electronic countermeasures. Flying above and providing advance early warning were the E-2C Hawkeyes of the VAW-124 Bear Aces.

One of the VF-41 veterans called the first strike a "Fallon-type" mission, the naval air station where the U.S. Navy's Top Gun and attack equivalent "Strike U" were found.

Twenty aircraft of Airwing 8 headed for fuel depots and ammunition-storage facilities ten miles north of Pristina. Each pilot wore "cats eye" night-vision goggles, and the F-14s were each equipped with LANTIRN (low altitude navigation and targeting infrared for night) pods, and every aircraft had forward-looking infrared (FLIR) cameras.

Due to an earlier clerical error putting the latitude and longitudinal codes into the aircraft's targeting computers, the strikes against the fuel depots were actually more than half a mile off course, but due to the quick thinking of *Desert Storm* veteran and F-14 Radar Intercept Officer (RIO) Lieutenant Commander Louis "Loose" Cannon, who was able to use a recognizable railroad track system, one of the F-14 strikers arrived at its allotted time on target (TOT) with seconds to spare. Dropping two 2,000lb GBU-16s, the laser-guided bombs found their desired mean point of impact (DMPI, pronounced "dimpy"), causing a massive explosion and fire that would burn for days. Secondary explosions occurred as the fuel depot erupted into fire and flame.

The second day of the war for Airwing 8 and VF-41and VF-14 saw further strikes against fuel storage facilities, but these were underground, causing the F-14s to carry larger GBU-24 penetrator bombs: 2,000lb bunker-busters designed to explode milliseconds after impact when the bomb had burrowed deep into the ground. The first night there had been incorrect coordinates put in; the second night two strikes dropped on the wrong target. The methods of modern warfare with all its technological advancement were proving more difficult than anticipated and still able to fall victim to human error.

Day two of the war for Airwing 8 also involved going after the fielded forces of the Serbian Army conducting the genocide in Kosovo. NATO and General Clark's decision to switch targets stemmed directly from the lack of impact the airstrikes were having in Serbia proper. Airwing 8 launched in the early morning hours of April 8 but returned with nothing to show for its efforts despite locating a tank and armored personnel carrier (APC), which it was unable to get permission to attack. Further strikes on the 8th and 9th were canceled due to weather. Robert K. Wilcox, author of *Black Aces*, noted that after multiple missed targets and missed opportunities, "It was not a happy ready room."

VF-41 and VF-14 returned to the fight on the 10th in a large Alpha strike with four Tomcats, two from each squadron, as the strikers and carrying GBU-10s. They were supported by F/A-18s as escorts, along with two EA-6Bs, and each of the Prowlers had an additional F-14 escort. A heavy thunderstorm nearly caused an abort, and although the F-14s of VF-41 did not drop their bombs, the Tomcats of VF-14 several miles in trail were able to prosecute the attack.

An F-14 awaits its catapult shot on board the USS *Theodore Roosevelt* in support of Operation *Noble Anvil*, the American portion of *Allied Force*. (DOD)

Over at Podgorica's Golubovci Airfield, the Serbian Air Force moved several Super Galeb attack aircraft. Golubovci was only 30 miles from the Albanian border, where the United States had placed 24 AH-64 Apache attack helicopters within striking distance of the Serbian Air Force should they decide to attack. General Clark and Lt Gen Short held a meeting along with Vice Admiral Daniel Murphy Jr, Commander Sixth Fleet. Clark, fearing an attack against the Apaches in Albania, queried Lt Gen Short about attacking the aircraft at Golubovci. Short, knowing it would take USAF assets three days to plan and conduct a strike, asked Admiral Murphy if the Navy could do the job. Fowler said he could. The strike would occur the same day: April 15.

This was not going to be an easy strike mission; the airfield was not only protected by SAMs, but the Galebs were packed tightly into a reinforced steel underground hangar. The underground hangar was connected to the main runway by a 3km-long taxiway, and was located adjacent to Sipcanik Hill, near the town of Tuzi. The hill doubled as an underground

PODGORICA AIR FORCE BASE, SERBIA
POST STRIKE

Although it is difficult to determine the damage done at the Podgorica Air Base in Serbia from the post-strike photo, the image clearly indicates the difficulty in targeting the air base facilities concealed in the natural terrain. (NATO/BELGA/AFP via Getty Images)

U.S. Navy "Alpha Strike" against Golubovci Air Base and Tuzi Hardenend Aircraft Shelter

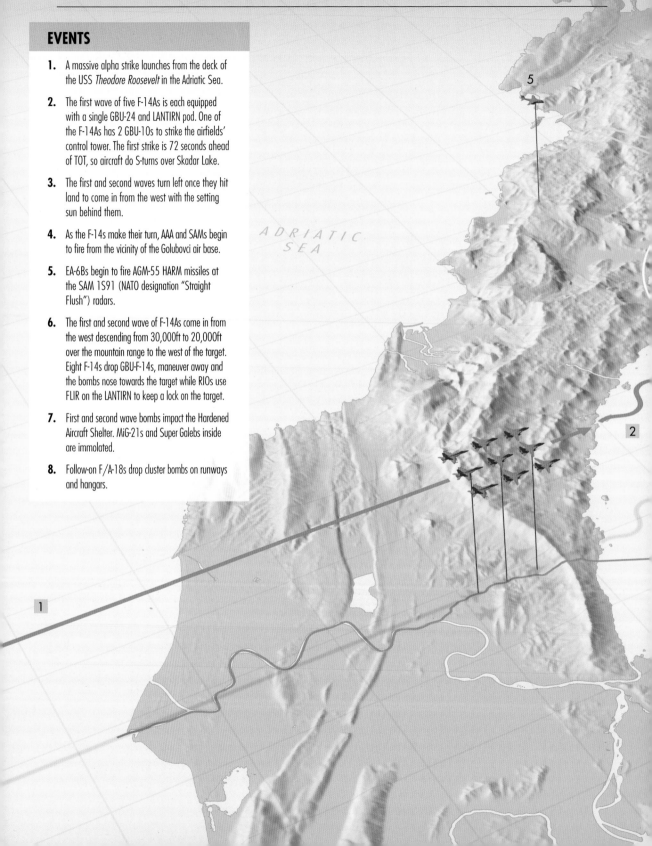

EVENTS

1. A massive alpha strike launches from the deck of the USS *Theodore Roosevelt* in the Adriatic Sea.

2. The first wave of five F-14As is each equipped with a single GBU-24 and LANTIRN pod. One of the F-14As has 2 GBU-10s to strike the airfields' control tower. The first strike is 72 seconds ahead of TOT, so aircraft do S-turns over Skadar Lake.

3. The first and second waves turn left once they hit land to come in from the west with the setting sun behind them.

4. As the F-14s make their turn, AAA and SAMs begin to fire from the vicinity of the Golubovci air base.

5. EA-6Bs begin to fire AGM-55 HARM missiles at the SAM 1S91 (NATO designation "Straight Flush") radars.

6. The first and second wave of F-14As come in from the west descending from 30,000ft to 20,000ft over the mountain range to the west of the target. Eight F-14s drop GBU-F-14s, maneuver away and the bombs nose towards the target while RIOs use FLIR on the LANTIRN to keep a lock on the target.

7. First and second wave bombs impact the Hardened Aircraft Shelter. MiG-21s and Super Galebs inside are immolated.

8. Follow-on F/A-18s drop cluster bombs on runways and hangars.

MONTENEGRO
ALBANIA

SHKODRA
LAKE

aircraft shelter. Forty aircraft, a true large-force employment mission or Alpha strike, was in the offing. The Tomcats and their LANTIRNs would strike the underground hangar at both ends and at its ventilation shaft using the GBU-24 bunker-busters. F/A-18 Hornets planned to carpet the runway with cluster bombs. EA-6Bs would fire HARMs at the SAM radars. The plan called for four waves to attack the airfield in what would be a continuous pounding for nearly 20 minutes.

The underground hangar took direct hits by no fewer than four of the GBU-24s and Super Galebs and MiG-21s parked inside were immolated. Despite the bombs aimed at the ventilation tunnel missing and the strikers missing the airfield tower, the raid was a resounding success. The Yugoslav-era aircraft hangar and underground bunker was later converted into a 356m-long tunnel, which now houses millions of gallons of wine and is a tourist destination in Montenegro. Despite these obvious successful attacks, Milosevic gave no indication of backing down and the air war dragged on.

Throughout the campaign the air wing of the *Roosevelt* launched over 3,100 sorties. Nearly half of all AGM-88 HARMs were fired by the EA-6Bs of the *Roosevelt*.

NATO bombing of Albanian refugees

Throughout the campaign and despite NATO's best efforts, bombs and missiles did kill innocent civilians. Outside agencies and non-governmental organizations (NGOs) recorded at least 15 such incidents during the conflict. Human Rights Watch estimated the number of civilian deaths and accidental attacks to be even higher, noting that more than 500 civilians died as a direct result of NATO bombing. Again, this should not take away from the precise nature of the campaign nor from NATO's efforts to limit collateral damage.

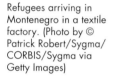

Refugees arriving in Montenegro in a textile factory. (Photo by © Patrick Robert/Sygma/ CORBIS/Sygma via Getty Images)

On April 14, NATO aircraft attacked a convoy of vehicles along a 12-mile stretch of road between the cities of Dečani and Đakovica, thinking it contained Yugoslav forces. More than a dozen aircraft, some of them American F-16s, were overhead during the attack. Given the desire to minimize civilian casualties and collateral damage, the pilots were undoubtedly

cleared to attack, either by a NATO E-3 AWACS or directly from operators on the floor of the CAOC. In reality, it was a refugee convoy. NATO bombs killed 73 Albanian refugees, including 16 children. After the attack, NATO leaders stated that the convoy had been military and the civilian deaths occurred in a massacre following the bombing. Two days later, NATO walked this statement back, admitting to the bombing of the refugee convoy.

On April 23, NATO aircraft attacked the Serb Radio and Television (RTS) headquarters in Belgrade. Debate between the United States and French planners had forced the date of the attack to slip from April 12 to the 23rd. Prior to the 12th, NATO had let it be known it considered the site to be a valid target and warned allied media and the Serbian government. Once the attack slipped more than a week, workers no longer considered the threat real and returned to work. The attack on the night of the 23rd killed 16 civilian workers and wounded an additional 16.

On May 13, and one month after the Dečani and Đakovica incidents, as many as 87 displaced Kosovar civilians were killed and 60 wounded when bombs were dropped during the night on a refugee camp in a wooded area on the Prizren–Suva Reka road, near the village of Korisa in Kosovo. There was a problem with this later attack. NATO leaders declared the site as a legitimate military target, with confirmation of a command post, armored personnel carriers, artillery, and other dug-in, concealed military positions. Why there were displaced Kosovars at this particular military encampment has never been established. It is possible that Yugoslav forces used the refugees as human shields, believing it would protect them from possible NATO air attacks despite this being directly forbidden by the Geneva Conventions.

Despite these and other civilian casualty incidents, Pentagon Spokesman Kenneth Bacon stated:

> This accident at Korisa did not shake NATO's resolve in any way…NATO deeply regrets civilian casualties…We try very hard to avoid these casualties, but combat is inherently dangerous and accidents cannot be avoided…this mission, like every other, will be reviewed, and the airmen and their commanders will learn what they can from it and continue. But I don't anticipate that there will be a sweeping change. We can't cross legitimate military targets off the list, and we won't.

A quagmire?

On April 23 in Washington, DC, senior leaders met at the NATO summit to commemorate NATO's 50th anniversary. Clearly, the conflict in Serbia and Kosovo was the most talked-about event. The first document to come out of the summit was a statement on Kosovo. NATO leaders reiterated their desire for the conflict to end, but also reiterated the steps Milosevic had to take for an end to the campaign to occur and that these oft-repeated requirements – including a stop to all military action in Kosovo and a withdrawal of forces from Kosovo – were non-negotiable. There would be "no compromise on these conditions." With the air campaign about to stretch into its third month, NATO leaders approved an intensification of air operations and widened the target list to include media targets and an expansion of military-industrial infrastructure targets. It seemed NATO leaders were becoming increasingly concerned with *Allied Force* developing into a quagmire.

Quagmire, the word so often associated with the conflict in Vietnam, began to surface. Democratic Senator Bill Bradley, a presidential candidate in the coming 2000 election, stated, "I fully support the American and NATO troops who are now in danger overseas. However, I have serious questions about our policy. We are escalating our commitment without establishing a clear exit strategy. As with Bosnia, we run the risk of becoming bogged down in a quagmire whose end we cannot predict or control." Republican Pat Buchanan stated, "There is no vital interest of the United States in that Balkan peninsula and whose flag flies over Pristina. There never has been. An American army has never fought there before."

Refugees cross the mountains on foot to arrive in Montenegro. (Photo by David Brauchli/ Sygma via Getty Images)

Others were not as pessimistic. Senator John McCain noted, "We must now do whatever it takes to win. We cannot allow this Balkan thug to prevail. We must do whatever is necessary, including perhaps sending in ground troops." Still, the lack of decisive gains frustrated General Clark, who asked for more air power to be sent into the region – an increase in the neighborhood of 300 more airplanes.

Senior leaders inside the DOD approved Clark's request. As part of that request and preceding the combat aircraft, the United States Secretary of Defense William Cohen ordered the deployment of an additional 30 air-to-air refuelers to pave the way and provide the necessary air-bridge to move the aircraft into theater. The additional KC-135s and KC-10s not only helped move more combat air power into theater; it also offered combat aircraft more refueling opportunities, and thus, more time on-station loitering over Serbia and Kosovo. This, again, was another indication that NATO continued to need to expand the air war.

Another condition that changed at this time was the delegation of the authorities needed to approve certain strikes. In essence, targets with the possibility of collateral damage like those inside Belgrade or other urban centers remained tightly controlled, but for those meeting preapproved criteria and of a more dynamic nature like forces in the field, the approval process was shifted to commanders in the field or in the CAOC.

Task Force Hawk

General Clark also asked for AH-64 Apaches. Since the attack helicopters were more closely associated with ground combat than with traditional air power, some worried this was the precursor to a land invasion by NATO forces. As mentioned above, on April 21 AH-64 Apache gunships arrived in Albania as part of Task Force Hawk. Although these aircraft never fired a round, their deployment became the source of much conjecture and study after the end of the conflict.

The root of the problem stemmed from doctrinal differences between the United States Army and the Air Force. From the perspective of the Army, Apache helicopters supported ground commanders and a wider land-centric effort. Without a supported land component, the Apaches would need to be commanded like other air assets and fall under the tactical command of Lt Gen Short at the Combined Air Operations Center. Lieutenant General John

Hendrix, commander of the task force, outright refused to have Army rotary wing assets fall under Air Force command or appear on the daily air-tasking order (ATO) which listed each day's pre-planned strikes. From Hendrix's perspective, Apaches did not strike pre-planned targets. They supported ground forces and looked for targets of opportunity. Essentially, Hendrix wanted an unfettered "hunting license" for the Apache pilots to roam free across the battlefield. Since Short and Hendrix were both three-star generals, the matter had to be routed up the chain for a decision by the Joint Chiefs of Staff (JCS) back in Washington.

The JCS invented a solution whereby the AH-64s did appear on the ATO, but Hendrix was given a "window" to operate when there would be no other allied aircraft striking targets in the area. The "solution" did not really matter, as the AH-64 Apaches of Task Force Hawk never appeared on the ATO and did not perform any missions in support of *Allied Force*. If anything, it proved there remained extreme dissension and parochial viewpoints among services about the roles and missions of differing air power platforms and assets.

Another problem that plagued Task Force Hawk was that it was not only a deployment of 24 Apaches. Task Force Hawk was a deployment of an entire U.S. Army Aviation Brigade Combat Team. Instead of two dozen helicopters, this included a brigade headquarters, a multiple-launch rocket system (MLRS) battalion, a ground maneuver brigade combat team, a corps support group, a signal battalion, a headquarters troop battalion, a military police detachment, a psychological operations detachment, and a special operations command-and-control element – a more significant deployment than was generally understood. The larger size of the deployment could not only send signals NATO might not intend, but it created a larger American footprint close to the Serbian border, which increased the opportunity for loss of NATO forces should Serbian forces move to a more offensive posture. As noted previously, the deployment of the Aviation Brigade Combat Team necessitated a short-notice, time-sensitive strike against the Golubovci Airfield.

A final reason that senior air commanders chose not to use the task force was undoubtedly their already successful record in suffering minimal aerial losses. The simple fact was that

An AH-64 Apache, part of Task Force Hawk, launches on a training sortie out of Rinas Airport in Albania. The Apaches flew no combat missions but did send the message that NATO was willing to escalate combat operations and perhaps even put NATO troops on the ground in Kosovo. (Mike Nelson/AFP via Getty Images)

A C-17 from Charleston AFB, South Carolina, delivers supplies for the AH-64 deployment of Task Force Hawk. (USAF)

by the time the task force was in place, NATO's only crewed loss was the F-117. However, NATO had lost several lower-flying UAVs, and the AH-64s were low-flying aircraft. Their use would certainly place them within easy reach of Serbian AAA and MANPADs. By not using the Apaches, NATO could preserve the idea that Serbian surface-to-air fire remained largely ineffective, but the loss of even one or two of the helicopters could rapidly change that perception in media and international circles.

NOVI SAD RADIO RELAY & TV-FM BROADCAST STATION, SERBIA

PRE STRIKE

POST STRIKE

Pre- and post-strike photos allowed NATO planners to define battle damage assessment and determine the progress of the ongoing operations. Here the Novi Sad Radio Relay and TV-FM broadcast station can be seen in both pre- and post-strike photos, and damage to the facility is obvious. (DOD/Getty Images)

Strikes continue

At the end of April, USAF Major General Charles Wald, the Vice Director for Strategic Plans and Policy on the Joint Staff, noted in one of his daily press briefings that although the weather was extremely poor and the worst he had seen in the area of operations, the only thing more persistent than the weather was "NATO's will to continue." As part of that will to continue, Wald briefed the assembled members of the press about the ongoing effort and showed numerous post-strike photos. One photo in particular showed the Pristina General Storage Deport in Kosovo. Wald noted that although the buildings themselves were intact, there were holes in two of the structures' roofs and that therefore they had been "rendered destroyed inside the buildings." He called these post-strike photos showing relatively intact buildings an "imagery interpretation problem."

Other strike photos shown at this briefing included the Sremcica radio relay station and the Prokuplje communications site in Serbia. This brief also provided several videos of American F-15Es dropping AGM-130 radar-guided bombs against the Krecedin Radar Site, the Pristina Airfield command post bunker, and the Novi Sad railway bridge. Each video, taken from a recording from the point of view of the weapon itself, showed the munition growing ever closer to its intended target before the screen went blank at impact. Based on the footage from the cameras on board the F-117s, laser-guided bombs struck a radio relay site, a TV-FM transmitter tower in Serbia, and a petroleum storage facility. The recording of the TV-FM strike was particularly impressive, as the assembled media clearly saw the tower topple after the bomb's explosion. In fighter pilot vernacular, this was a "shack" or direct hit. Each of these strikes took place between April 21 and 25.

May: NATO escalation

One month into the campaign, NATO planners seemed inclined to take the gloves off and step up attacks against Milosevic's backers. Targets now included: oil refineries; petroleum, oil, and lubricant (POL) storage facilities; rail and bridges over the Danube; and other military industrial targets. At the end of April, NATO decided to turn off the televisions in Belgrade and strike targets of Milosevic's political supporters. The attack against the headquarters of Serbian radio and television killed more than a dozen civilians, and Amnesty International called it a war crime, despite NATO's warnings that they viewed the station as a valid military target. Other regime-supporting targets included transmission towers and radio control buildings. As one NATO member noted, "Two nights ago we attacked the brains behind the brutality in Belgrade and yesterday we went after the nervous system that keeps the Milosevic machine informed and in touch." For the first time, Milosevic's staunchest allies and supporters and the machine used to keep him in power fell under NATO air attack. While Milosevic himself was never targeted, one of the national command centers was destroyed by a GBU-37, a bomb weighing 4,700lb and capable of deep penetration underground.

On May 3, an attack carried out by American F-117s dropped BLU-114Bs inside Belgrade on the electrical power grid. The bombs released spools of graphite-filament fibers that, upon coming into contact with electrical stations, short-circuited the system and turned off the electricity. As much as 70 percent of Serbia lost power after this attack. While the main purpose of the attack was to disrupt military communications, it undoubtedly sent signals to Milosevic's supporters that the noose was continuing to tighten.

Although the television/radio tower remains standing near Vranje, Serbia, it is doubtful that it can send or receive information, as the rubble-strewn ground indicates that support facilities around the tower are now standing after a NATO strike. (Scott Peterson/Liaison/Getty Images)

Another shot of munitions ready for action. Here on the wing of an RNLAF F-16AM you can see two AIM-9 sidewinder missiles and one CBU unit. (USAF)

Milosevic's fielded forces operating from Kosovo also came under more attacks. NATO had refined its targeting to two primary sets: first, Milosevic's political power along with his command control apparatus, and second, his fielded forces. These two sets now became the primary centers of gravity that NATO air planners set about to put the most pressure on. One of the heaviest raids of the war was launched on the evening of May 10, when a mixed package of B-52s and B-1Bs departed using call signs Havoc 11-14, Razor 11-12, and Titus 41-42 struck targets in both Kosovo and Serbia.

NATO strike aircraft went after the full array of Serbian fielded forces: artillery guns, tanks, armored personnel carriers, mortars, military vehicles, artillery rocket systems, command posts, and local ammunition and fuel supplies. However, Serbian air defense systems remained active and a threat as the commander of the 555th Fighter Squadron discovered on May 2.

Hammer 34 rescue

On May 2 at 0200hrs local time, a four-ship formation of U.S. F-16CGs from the 555th "Triple Nickle" Fighter Squadron out of Aviano Air Base was on a SEAD mission. The four-ship's call sign was "Hammer," and the squadron commander of that unit was Lieutenant Colonel David "Fingers" Goldfein. That day Goldfein was "Hammer 34." As the four-ship entered into the area, it immediately came under AAA fire. As Hammer 1 and 2 attacked the AAA, 3 called, "Hammer 3 is defending 060 mud," which indicated they were being targeted by a Serbian SA-3 battery.

One of these surface-to-air missiles proximity fused and exploded behind Goldfein's aircraft, prompting the pilot to inform the rest of the flight: "Mud, 3 just took a hit… engines running…I'm headed west 190. Shit, Okay, I've got vibrations. Hammer 3 [sic] has got problems…got engine problems. I took a hit and I'll be getting out of the airplane. I'm going to continue to glide as long as I can." Goldfein noted there had been a "big flash, loud explosion," but he did not have time to panic and was later praised for his calmness under the duress of the situation.

Goldfein then told the other aircraft, "Start finding me boys." With these words, Goldfein set into motion another combat search and rescue. In the aircraft, Goldfein did all he could to restart the aircraft and get the engine running but to avail. Goldfein wryly remarked,

"I'm a glider." Hammer 3 was able to visually track his wingman's aircraft through the cloud deck. Even before ejecting, the CSAR effort was already underway as the "Magic" AWACS began to coordinate Hammer 34's rescue. Inside the stricken aircraft, the squadron commander squared away his interior, putting away any loose items lest they become shrapnel, removed his night vision goggles, reached down, and pulled his ejection handles. Unfortunately, for Goldfein, his parachute was not a dark green combat color but a dayglow orange training parachute, which shone brightly in the moonlight and alerted any Serbian forces in the area to his exact location. Once on the ground, Goldfein started to maneuver away from his landing area, concealed some of survival gear, located what he believed to be an appropriate rescue area, and settled in to wait.

At Tuzla Air Base in Bosnia, the AFSOC 55th Special Operations Squadron received the notification an F-16 had been shot down, but the pilot had safely ejected. Much like the rescue of Vega-31, the rescue of Hammer 34 began in earnest. A rescue force of one MH-53 Pave Low and two MH-60 Pave Hawks lifted off. The rescue force came under heavy Serbian attack from AAA and surface-to-air missiles while flying only 50 to 100ft from the ground. Both sides knew what was at stake and both sides tried desperately to be the first to find the downed aviator.

Meanwhile, A-10 "Sandys," serving as the on-sight command-and-control element, maintained contact with Goldfein and talked the rescue force toward their location. Finally spying Goldfein's rescue strobe, the Pave Low set down and three pararescuemen hopped out to retrieve the pilot, but the Serbians refused to give up their prize without a fight and fired at the rescue force with small arms. Once aboard the aircraft, the pararescuemen piled on top of Goldfein as the rescue force blazed a trail for the relative safety of Bosnian air space.

Serbian air losses			
RV I PVO loss	Downed by	Munition used	Date
MiG-29	American F-15C	AIM-120	March 24
MiG-29	American F-15C	AIM-120	March 24
MiG-29	RNLAF F-16AM	AIM-120	March 24
MiG-29 x 2	F-15C	AIM-120	March 26
MiG-29	F-16CJ	AIM-120	May 4

AN MH-53J Pave Low helicopter rescued downed squadron commander Lt Col Dave Goldfein after his F-16 was shot down. Goldfein went on to become the USAF Chief of Staff and recognized the heroism of his rescue crew every year after his rescue. (USAF)

Hammer 34 rescue

1

CROATIA

BOSNIA

6

9

8

11

10

7

EVENTS

1. On 2 May, 1999 "Hammer Flight" a four ship of F-16CGs of the 555th Fighter Squadron engage against surface to air missiles of the 250th Air Defense Brigade and AAA. Hammer 34 is piloted by the squadron commander Lt. Col. David Goldfein.

2. Hammer 31 attacks AAA 15 miles west of Novi Sad. Hammer 32 provides support. Two other F-16 CGs continue to fly south.

3. Although receiving radar warning of ground threats, Lt. Col. David Goldfein doesn't receive a launch indication, nor does he visually see the missile.

4. Hammer 34 is struck by a SA-3 fired from the vicinity of the town of Karlovcic. Goldfein's F-16CG is on a heading of 120 at 19.5ft.

5. Goldfein turns to 250 in an attempt to escape Serbia and head to Bosnia. The entire Hammer flight flies 240 while trying to monitor Goldfein's progress. Hammer 34's engine cuts out.

6. Hammer 34 descends in his "glider", receiving AAA. He continues to bank the aircraft to 210. He passes 6,000ft at "Bullseye 232 for 28." He is 30 – 50 miles west of Belgrade.

2

3

5

4

SERBIA

BELGRADE

7. Hammer 34 ejects at 45,000ft and the F-16 crashes on the slopes of Mt. Cer.

8. A rescue force including 3x F-16CGs of Hammer Flight, 4x F-16CJs, and 1 ABCCC orbit overhead while the downed pilot maneuvers on the ground.

9. A combat search and rescue force CSAR of 4x A-10 "Sandys", 2x MH-53, and 1x MH-60G enter Serbian airspace at 0355hrs. They initially have trouble locating Goldfein who activates his infrared strobe.

10. They locate the downed pilot at 0441hrs, land at 0445hrs, and the extraction begins. Overhead the A-10s set up a Lufberry circle.

11. Goldfein is kneeling in a creek bed, just outside some trees. The pararescuemen authenticate him, put him in the helicopter and cover his body as Serbian forces engage with the rescue force.

NATO's final air-to-air victory

The final aerial victory came on May 4, when Lieutenant Colonel Michael "Dog" Geczy of the 78th Fighter Squadron flying an F-16CJ, call sign PUMA 11, shot down the fifth and final MiG-29 of the war. Geczy's four-ship of F-16CJs was part of a larger multinational strike package of British, Dutch, and French aircraft. That day the F-16CJs were loaded out with two AGM-55 HARMs, two AIM-120 AMRAAMs, and two AIM-9M sidewinders. In this instance, the F-16s of the 78th Fighter Squadron served to protect the strike force against both air-to-air and air-to-ground threats. As weather rolled in, the British and Dutch aircraft aborted their mission, but the American F-16CJs stayed with the French strikers. As the attack aircraft rolled out after dropping their bombs, an E-3 AWACS alerted the strike package to the presence of a single airborne MiG-29 (Colonel Milenko Pavlovic of the 204th Fighter Regiment, 127th Fighter Squadron). Colonel Pavlovic's target was not the French or American strike package; rather he was heading toward an RAF E-3D sentry of the No. 23 Squadron. Pavlovic flew treetop level and popped up to attempt to get a missile lock on the E-3. Despite being short on gas, Geczy and his wingman, First Lieutenant "DBAL" Austin, turned toward the threat. At 1246hrs, Geczy launched two AMRAAM missiles and both tracked to impact the MiG-29. Colonel Pavlovic did not survive the engagement. Lieutenant Colonel Geczy noted that as both missiles came off the rails, their fins turned, and both missiles dove with "rapid, arching attacks...like a pitcher throwing a curveball."

Geczy's aerial victory proved to be the last manned air-to-air combat kill for an American for almost the next two decades; not until June 18, 2017, with the shoot-down of a Syrian Su-22 fighter jet by a Navy F/A-18 Super Hornet, did American pilots engage in crewed aerial combat again.

Three American F-15Cs and one American F-16CJ accounted for five MiG-29 kills, and one Royal Netherlands F-16AM increased the total to six aerial victories, each one of them occurring against the MiG-29s of the 127th Fighter Squadron. All NATO aircraft used the AIM-120 AMRAAMs to kill their respective MiGs, indicating longer-distance kills than *Desert Storm*, when AIM-7s and AIM-9s also brought down Iraqi aircraft.

Bombing of the Chinese Embassy

One of the more unusual events of the war occurred on May 7, when an American B-2 Spirit dropped five JDAMs on the Chinese Embassy. Both immediately after the event and in the more than 20 years since the attack, there has been much discussion and argument about how the United States could possibly misidentify a foreign nation's embassy as a legitimate target. While some have characterized it as not an accident, an equal number pointed out that many older maps did not note that location as that of the Chinese Embassy. Complicating the matter even further was that this particular strike had the aid of the American Central Intelligence Agency (CIA).

Since it was B-2 Spirits which carried out the attack, some in NATO were quick to point out that these strategic assets were operating through an American-only chain of command. However, at the headquarters

The F-16CJ was the USAF's SEAD aircraft in *Allied Force*, equipped with specialist avionics and carrying either HARM or Shrike anti-radiation missiles. The variant had taken over the role from the recently retired F-4G Wild Weasel. (USAF)

in Brussels, NATO officials stated that every target was "meticulously planned." This particular attack did occur on a night where NATO strikes ramped up considerably and included the Dobanovci command complex and paramilitary group using the Hotel Yugoslavia as barracks. It is entirely possible that emissions coming from the Hotel Yugoslavia could have been interpreted as coming from the buildings of the embassy. Thus, when one considers outdated maps being used to identify supposedly empty buildings that were actively emitting military communications across the street from the known location of Serbian paramilitary forces, it is not a stretch to see how the accident occurred.

Turning out the lights

On May 24, rather than dropping the BLU-114Bs with their graphite fiber filaments, NATO dropped PGMs on the electrical power grid. This time the lights stayed off. This attack was followed shortly thereafter by a full-scale counteroffensive by the KLA. Although talk often centered on the use of NATO troops as ground forces, it almost ignored that the KLA represented a viable Serbian counterforce in the region. As the KLA attacked, Serbian forces massed to defeat them, and although the KLA rapidly moved to being on the defensive, the massing of the Serbian fielded forces was exactly the move NATO needed to find, fix, and attack the Serbian Army on the ground. Although Serbian forces did attempt to move in small groups, fighter and UAV forward air controllers (FACs) often found them, and this opened the Serbs up to ruthless attacks from the air.

Perhaps nothing signified a massive change in battlefield operations more than the use of the RQ-1 Predator reconnaissance unmanned aerial vehicles during the *Allied Force* operation. No one could know at the time just how ubiquitous the "drones" would become in modern warfare. One humorous story shows how the attack aircraft, the drone pilots, and the higher headquarters could not view ongoing combat operations. A lone RQ-1 Predator flew high over the Kosovo battlefield looking for enemy activity or movement. On the ground below, a lone Serbian tank sat nestled in a semi-hidden position all but invisible except to the drone operating overhead. The RQ-1's live video feed was seen in real time in both the air operations center in Vicenza, Italy, as well as in the allied headquarters in

A plethora of munitions, along with two S-3 Vikings, sit on the elevator and await loading on board the USS *Theodore Roosevelt*. Note the AIM-9 missiles and AGM-65 Mavericks have their sensitive infrared systems covered. (U.S. Navy/ Getty Images)

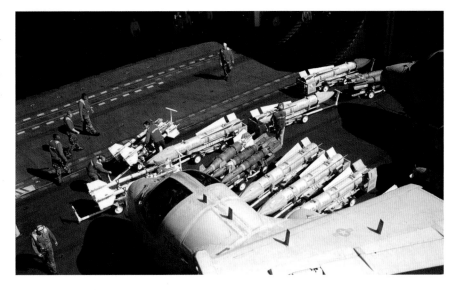

Mons, Belgium. This allowed both the senior air commander, Lt Gen Mike Short, and Supreme Allied Commander in Europe, General Wesley Clark, to observe the feed in real time. The two most senior commanders running the war were now able to view a tactical-level battlefield feed from the comforts of their command centers. Between the tank and the orbiting RQ-1 was a lone A-10. In his single-seat cockpit, Captain Chris "Junior" Short was receiving instructions from members of the CAOC, who attempted to direct him to the tank in order to destroy it. However, Captain Short's view was vastly different from the highly focused view of the RQ-1. It was proving to be something of an intractable situation.

As the story goes, General Wesley Clark called Lt Gen Short and told him to tell the CAOC to tell Captain Short to kill the tank. The CAOC dutifully relayed the message from their seats to an orbiting EC-130E airborne battlefield command and control center (ABCCC). The EC-130E radioed to Capt Short that the air component commander, Lt Gen Short, wanted Capt Short in his A-10 to kill the tank – the tank that the A-10 pilot was just as positive he could not find. The EC-130 called to Captain Short, telling him the general "… really wants you to find and kill that tank." Junior replied, "Tell my Dad I can't find the fucking tank!" Lieutenant General Short later denied this event ever occurred during an official oral history interview.

An F-16 from the Royal Danish Air Force is equipped with both AIM-9 and AIM-120 missiles, indicating that it is ready for a combat air patrol. (USAF)

KLA offensive and NATO air attacks

One of Serbia's biggest assets in hindering allied attacks was the weather itself. Throughout the entire 78-day campaign, only 24 days saw weather not play a factor in operations. One article pointed out later that there was 50 percent cloud cover over Serbia for 70 percent of the campaign, but the weather cleared on June 7. As Serbian forces launched another offensive against

KLA forces, the improved weather allowed two B-52s and two B-1Bs to drop a combined 86 general-purpose MK-82 and cluster bombs on the site where the Serbian forces massed. Of the more than 1,000 Serbian troops at the site, less than half of them survived. However, after 78 days of bombing, the air campaign was coming to an end.

In late May, the Kosovo Liberation Army went on the offensive. Later news reports stated that the offensive was conducted in conjunction with American and British intelligence agencies. Once the KLA came out to fight, the Yugoslav Army moved into the open and massed its formations in order to retaliate. Coincidentally, the weather over Kosovo also cleared. The weather and the massing of Yugoslav forces proved a perfect combination for NATO air power. American General Hugh Shelton noted, "You can see almost exponentially it starts to go up, to the point that when we suspended (attacks) we were up to 450 artillery and mortar pieces, approximately, about 220 armored personnel carriers and we're up around 120 tanks."

A victim of NATO airstrikes. The buckled remnants of a bridge over the Danube in the city of Novi Sad. Attacks like these not only hindered Serbian troop movements, but kept the civilian populace from crossing as well. NATO hoped strikes like these would place pressure on Milosevic to stop his ethnic cleansing efforts. (SERBIAN TV/AFP via Getty Images)

Weapons of *Allied Force*		
Range	Guidance	Weapon Name
Long	GPS	Tomahawk TLAM
Long	GPS	CALCM (AGM-86C)
Standoff	INS/GPS	SLAM (AGM-84E)
Standoff	Terminal	AGM-130
Standoff	GPS	JSOW (AGM-154)
Standoff	Terminal	Have Nap (AGM-142)
Standard bomb	GPS	JDAM (GBU-31)
Standard bomb	GPS	GBU-37
Standard bomb		Maverick (AGM-65)
Standard bomb	LGB	GBU-10, GBU-12, GBU-16, GBU-24, GBU-27, GBU-28
Standard bomb	Unguided	MK-82, MK-83, MK-84, BLU-109, CBU-87, CBU-99

Milosevic concedes

Milosevic finally agreed to withdraw his forces from Kosovo, in large part because of diplomatic pressure from Russia, and NATO suspended the bombing campaign on June 10. One question that continues to be asked is why Milosevic surrendered when he did. There are multiple answers, or rather multiple considerations that might have forced the Serbian leader's hand. For starters, there was no indication that the bombing campaign was going to let up in any measurable way. Although air campaign planners continued to have problems locating and attacking Serbian fielded forces, continued pounding of targets in and around Serbia was certainly at the forefront of Milosevic's mind.

A second problem faced by Milosevic was his loss of all international support in the face of what one study called the "sheer depravity of Serbia's conduct in Kosovo." Even Russia, Serbia's longtime ally, could no longer ignore the atrocities being committed. With the

One of the key reasons Milosevic conceded was not only the ongoing air campaign, but also the growing number of forces in NATO's Kosovo Force (KFOR) that continued to build up around Serbia and Kosovo during the campaign. While bombs rained down on his forces, NATO slowly began building up a force capable of a significant ground intervention should it become necessary. Here soldiers from the 5th Hafenumschlags Kompanie disembark at Salonica harbour in Greece. (Eric Feferberg/AFP via Getty Images)

complete removal of any international support, Serbia stood alone against not just NATO, but the entire international community.

Finally, Milosevic faced what was quickly turning from a possibility into a probability: a ground invasion in addition to the air strikes. With nearly 50,000 NATO troops located in Bosnia and Herzegovina as part of the NATO stabilization force, 7,500 troops in Albania, and an additional 8,000 in Macedonia, Milosevic could no longer deny the probability that NATO could intervene even further. In late May, President Bill Clinton twice indicated that he no longer ruled out "other military options," indicating the possibility of a NATO and American invasion into Kosovo. By the end of May 1999, it was readily apparent that NATO was preparing for a ground invasion in the event that its air campaign failed to end in capitulation.

In June, a Russian diplomatic team met with Milosevic in Belgrade, leading to the concession that all Serbian troops would be withdrawn from Kosovo, that Kosovo would be overseen by UN peacekeeping forces, and that Kosovo would not immediately seek independence. The bombing stopped on June 10. Despite the loss of Russian support and the growing

Two U.S. Navy Sikorsky CH-53 Sea Stallions depart the airport at Tirana, Albania, after the delivery of humanitarian aid for Kosovo refugees who fled their country and crossed into Albania seeking protection and shelter. The image of Kosovo refugees in neighboring countries galvanized global opposition to Milosevic. (Thomas Coex/AFP via Getty Images)

threat of a land invasion, it is very probable that NATO's continuous air offensive finally convinced Milosevic that forces aligned against him had the ability, the desire, the motive, and the backing to continue the air war, at least for the foreseeable future. The ceaseless bombing efforts running around the clock – although by no means the only factor responsible for the success of *Allied Force* – did play a decisive role leading to Milosevic's capitulation. In the end, Milosevic had nothing to gain and everything to lose by continuing to hold out against a growing global call for his surrender.

A Human Rights Watch report noted that at the end of hostilities, "By early June 1999, more than 80 percent of the entire population of Kosovo and 90 percent of Kosovar Albanians were displaced from their home." Yugoslav forces had successfully removed or forced to flee over 860,000 Albanians from Kosovo.

With hostilities ending on June 10, 1999, KFOR troops rushed into Kosovo. Here British troops have just left the two Chinook helicopters. For reasons unknown, these British troops followed on the heels of their American allies, according to British media reports. (Kevin Capon/Pool/AFP via Getty Images)

An American report after the war noted that the answer to the question of why Milosevic conceded when he did will never be conclusively answered, but did explore several potential factors. These included: the intensified air campaign; the alliance's continued efforts to engage Russia in diplomacy, which eventually proved critical to ending the conflict; the growing amount of ground forces in the region, indicating that a ground component of the conflict had moved from a possibility to a probability; the offensive of the Kosovo Liberation Army in the final days of the conflict; and other economic and political pressures, which all added together to eventually force Milosevic's hand.

NATO's bombing effort in the end played the determining role in bringing about Milosevic's defeat, but was it decisive? That depends on whom you ask. As noted at the beginning of this book, eminent historian John Keegan stated rather unequivocally, "Now there is a new turning point to fix on the calendar: June 3, 1999, when the capitulation of President Milosevic proved that war can be won by air power alone." This seems, in retrospect, and given the intervening almost 25 continuous years of conflict in Iraq, Afghanistan, Syria, and Libya, that while perhaps the single most important component of Milosevic's capitulation, air power was, once again, one of many tools used during *Allied Force* to gain a political outcome for NATO and the United Nations.

On June 9, 1999, the Federal Republic of Yugoslavia, the Republic of Serbia, and the NATO-led Kosovo Force signed the Kumanovo Agreement, also called the "Military Technical Agreement," ending NATO's bombing campaign and the wider war in Kosovo. It stated:

> The State Governmental authorities of the Federal Republic of Yugoslavia and the Republic of Serbia understand and agree that the international security force ("KFOR") will deploy following the adoption of the UNSCR referred to in paragraph 1 and operate without hindrance within Kosovo and with the authority to take all necessary action to establish and maintain a secure environment for all citizens of Kosovo and otherwise carry out its mission. They further agree to comply with all of the obligations of this Agreement and to facilitate the deployment and operation of this force.
>
> The FRY Forces shall immediately, upon entry into force (EIF) of this Agreement, refrain from committing any hostile or provocative acts of any type against any person in Kosovo and will order armed forces to cease all such activities. They shall not encourage, organise or support hostile or provocative demonstrations.

Phased Withdrawal of FRY Forces (ground): The FRY agrees to a phased withdrawal of all FRY Forces from Kosovo to locations in Serbia outside Kosovo. FRY Forces will mark and clear minefields, booby traps and obstacles. As they withdraw, FRY Forces will clear all lines of communication by removing all mines, demolitions, booby traps, obstacles and charges. They will also mark all sides of all minefields. International security forces' ("KFOR") entry and deployment into Kosovo will be synchronized.

This included withdrawal of the Yugoslavia Air and Air Defense Forces as well.

The United States Department of Defense held a press briefing on June 10 that detailed in its entirety the phases of the NATO air and missile war against Serbian and Yugoslav forces, noting that the campaign proceeded from "set conditions" to "isolate" and then on to "decimate." Under each of the cloud-shaped phases were lines showing which phase they occurred in. For example, "IADS" was found in all three phases, while industry and power were only in the "decimate" stage. However for a campaign that was supposed to last only 72 hours, the briefing seemed to indicate that the U.S. and its NATO allies had been prepared from the outset for a lengthier campaign.

Pristina airport incident

One conflict remained to be settled. On June 12, a Russian military force headed off for Pristina Airport in order to set up police activity. General Clark viewed this as the Russians taking advantage of NATO's hard-won victory. Clark ordered British General Michael David Jackson to take the Kosovo Force and get to the airport before the Russians. Jackson refused, stating, "I'm not going to start the Third World War for you." Instead, the KFOR surrounded the airport in what became a tense two-week standoff, before a settlement was reached and the Russians were integrated into the peacekeeping operations, but not under NATO control.

Although the aims and objectives of the campaign were achieved, it took significantly longer than NATO and American air planners initially believed. The analysis and conclusion will also discuss just how decisive air power was in forcing Milosevic to comply with NATO demands.

Newly arrived Russian forces make their way along the main Belgrade-Pristina highway towards the airport. (Photo by MIKE NELSON/AFP via Getty Images)

Statistics

On June 21, U.S. Secretary of Defense William Cohen announced during a press briefing that he had just ordered General Clark to begin the redeployment of more than 300 combat

aircraft back to their home bases. Cohen, noting that the conflict was over, called it the "most precise air campaign in history." Interestingly, Cohen noted that more than 47,000 Serbian military and police forces and over 800 tanks, armored personnel carriers, and AAA pieces departed the Kosovo autonomous region. This clearly indicated the still significant strength the Serbians had inside Kosovo at the end of hostilities.

During the entirety of the operation, NATO aircrews flew 38,004 sorties over the course of the 78-day campaign. The total number of actual strike sorties was 10,484. Perhaps the most impressive statistic to come out of the operation from the NATO perspective was that

throughout the 78 days of the campaign and the entirety of the attack missions, there were no NATO combat fatalities.

A B-1B Lancer from Ellsworth Air Force Base, South Dakota, lands after a Kosovo mission at RAF Fairford, England, April 28, 1999. (USAF/AFP via Getty Images)

Human rights aftermath

History will resist efforts to assign a definitive total to the number of those killed in the ethnic cleansing that occurred between March and June 1999. Little doubt exists that the Serbian government intentionally destroyed any records or evidence of their atrocities. A generally accepted number seems to be between 7,000 and 13,000 ethnic Albanians killed between March and June; thousands of bodies were exhumed from mass graves in the aftermath of the conflict, and thousands more remained missing, almost all of them ethnic Albanians. Serbian forces targeted and killed individually many supporters of the KLA or those in support of Kosovo independence. This is to say nothing of the rapes and sexual assaults that occurred. One report noted that Serbian and Yugoslav forces used rape "…deliberately as an instrument to terrorize the civilian population, extort money from families, and push people to flee their homes. Rape also furthered the goal of forcing ethnic Albanians from Kosovo." The Human Rights Watch found nearly 100 credible cases of rape occurring in the first six months of 1999.

Allies and air power

The Chairman of the American Joint Chiefs of Staff, General Henry H. Shelton, in the official American after-action report, said this about the air war in Kosovo:

> A turning point in NATO's long and successful history, Operation *Allied Force* was an overwhelming success. We forced Slobodan Milosevic to withdraw his forces from Kosovo, degraded his ability to wage military operations, and rescued over one million refugees. We accomplished these goals through a cohesive alliance of democratic nations whose military men and women conducted the most effective air operation in history.

Air component commander Lieutenant General Michael Short spoke disparagingly about the allied effort, suggesting that the U.S. contribution far surpassed that of other NATO nations. After the war, he said, "I don't think there's any question that we've got an A team and a B team now" and that some NATO members were "relegated to doing nothing but flying combat air patrol in the daytime; that's all they were capable of doing." Short went even further, noting that some NATO countries "are on the second team, and they know that." He also criticized foreign pilots as possibly posing a language barrier during combat operations.

A report issued in 2000 by the American Department of Defense was clearly meant to walk back Short's insult to NATO allies, saying that "our NATO allies were crucial partners and contributors throughout the operation. Our European allies' aircraft that were committed to the operation were roughly as large a part of their total inventory of aircraft as was the case for the United States, and they flew a very substantial number of strike missions, facing the same dangers as U.S. aircrews." Furthermore, while the United States did provide the preponderance of air assets, this same report noted that the European allies provided the majority of human relief workers and supplies.

Short's comments did highlight some of the problems of a lack of interoperability among the NATO members. One air power historian noted several areas in which the United States and the other allies could not conduct operations together. This included secure telephone communications and a lack of frequency-hopping ultra-high frequency (UHF) radios in their aircraft for encrypted communications (causing NATO E-3 AWACS to transmit "in the clear" and thus be detectable by enemy forces on the ground listening in).

Among all participants, only U.S., British, Canadian, and French aircraft had the ability to deliver precision-guided munitions or laser-guided bombs. All of this forced Lt Gen Short to later admit that he could not "risk sending the aircraft of many countries into harm's way because of concern for their safety." Whether this was true or what the other allied nations viewed as typical American bluster and over-compensation remains open to debate and interpretation. The same report mentioned above also noted that all of these deficiencies placed a "disproportionate burden of responsibility for combat operations to the United States and impeded our ability to operate more effectively with NATO allies." This is in opposition to what Lt Gen Short said, indicating that the United States had inadvertently placed the burden on themselves rather than the fault lying with the other NATO members.

Often lost in histories of air campaigns or larger conflicts is the work of the air mobility pilots. Americans of the Air Mobility Command flew 2,130 airlift missions throughout *Allied Force* and moved 32,111 passengers in and around the region and delivered 52,645 short tons of cargo. Aerial tankers flew over 9,000 sorties and delivered 348 million pounds of fuel.

Not all naval support came from the "big" aircraft carriers. AV-8B Harrier attack aircraft like the one seen here launched from smaller Tarawa-class amphibious assault ships. This Harrier is preparing to launch from the USS *Nassau*. Note the aircraft is carrying traditional "gravity bombs" which required precision delivery as opposed to newer precision-guided variants. (U.S. Navy/Getty Images)

AFTERMATH AND ANALYSIS

General Wesley Clark supposedly stated of Operation *Allied Force*: "This was the only campaign in history in which lovers strolled down riverbanks in the gathering twilight and ate at outdoor cafes and watched the fireworks." Interestingly enough, a month after the treaty was signed, General Clark received a phone call from Chairman of the Joint Chiefs of Staff, General Hugh Shelton, notifying Clark that he was being relieved earlier than his full three-year tour. Many see this as a type of retribution, although Clark stated it was a routine action. Some saw the firing of Clark as the last bomb dropped in the conflict.

Milosevic remained in power until September 2000, when he lost the majority vote in an election he himself had called. Refusing to relinquish power, Milosevic hoped the JNA and its leaders would remain loyal to him, but in this belief, he was wrong. Without the support of his military commanders, Milosevic accepted defeat on October 6, 2000.

Just six months later, on April 1, 2001, Yugoslav authorities arrested Slobodan Milosevic. For 36 hours, Yugoslav police forces surrounded and participated in a standoff between police and Milosevic's bodyguards at his Belgrade villa. On June 28, Yugoslav leaders had Milosevic extradited to the International Criminal Tribunal for the former Yugoslavia (ICTY) at The Hague, Netherlands.

On March 11, 2006, Milosevic was found dead in his prison cell in the UN War Crimes Tribunal's detention center. He was later found guilty of numerous crimes against humanity. One of the verdicts released in 2007 noted:

> Between 1991 and 1995, Martić held positions of minister of interior, minister of defense and president of the self-proclaimed "Serbian Autonomous Region of Krajina" (SAO Krajina), which was later renamed "Republic of Serbian Krajina" (RSK). He was found to have participated during this period in a joint criminal enterprise which included Slobodan Milošević, whose aim was to create a unified Serbian state through commission of a widespread and systematic campaign of crimes against non-Serbs inhabiting areas in Croatia and Bosnia and Herzegovina envisaged to become parts of such a state.

A Royal Norwegian Air Force F-16A drops away after refueling over the Balkan region from a United States Air Force KC-135R of the 22nd Air Refueling Wing. (USAF)

In a 2021 verdict, the International Residual Mechanism for Criminal Tribunals noted that:

> The Trial Chamber, therefore, finds proven beyond reasonable doubt that, from at least August 1991, and at all times relevant to the crimes charged in the Indictment, a common criminal purpose existed to forcibly and permanently remove, through the commission of the crimes of persecution, murder, deportation and inhumane acts (forcible transfer), the majority of non-Serbs, principally Croats, Bosnian Muslim and Bosnian Croats, from large areas of Croatia and Bosnia and Herzegovina. The Trial Chamber finds that the common criminal purpose, as defined above, was shared by senior political, military, and police leadership in Serbia, the SAO Krajina, the SAO SBWS, and Republika Srpska, with the core members, among others and varying depending on the area and timing of the commission of the crimes, being Slobodan Milošević.

A group of Kosovar children, one waving the American flag, greet members of the KFOR as they arrive in Kosovo. Although the campaign was not over yet, when these troops arrived on June 1, 1999, Milosevic's options of anything other than surrender and compliance with NATO were rapidly dwindling. (Patrick Aventurier/ Gamma-Rapho via Getty Images)

Final thoughts and the impact of air power

Although it may never be decided if air power alone won *Allied Force*, it is worth planting a flag somewhere on the usefulness and overall contributions of air power in this particular conflict. A dug-in and intractable enemy. A difficult and impenetrable terrain. A region and weather ill-suited for the best practices of air power application. How useful was air power during this particular operation? Some might see the relative ease of victory in *Desert Storm* and view air power's results in Serbia as something *less*. The opposite is true. Despite the enemy, the terrain, and the weather, air power proved strategically, operationally, and tactically successful. Even more so than in *Desert Storm*.

American air power theorist and practitioner Brigadier General Billy Mitchell said in his most famous work, *Winged Defense: The Development and Possibilities of Modern Air Power: Economic and Military*, that "air power is the ability to do something in the air." This was later amended by others to "air power is the ability to do something *strategically* useful in the air." Italian theorist, and Mitchell's contemporary, Giulio Douhet, stated in *The Command of the Air*, "To conquer the command of the air means victory; to be beaten in the air means defeat and acceptance of whatever terms the enemy may be pleased to impose." Douhet's quote strikes truer in the case of Operation *Allied Force*. Milosevic had no ability to stand against the combined might of NATO air power. In that sense, he was beaten before the first bomb was dropped. Air power theorist Alexander de Seversky stated, "The actual elimination or even stalemating of an attacking air force can be achieved only by a superior air force." NATO used its own air power to stalemate and defeat the Yugoslav Air Force. Admiral Lord Jack Fisher said, "As the locusts swarmed over Egypt, so will aircraft swarm in the heavens, carrying inconceivable cargoes of men and bombs, some fast and some slow." NATO aircraft certainly fit this bill.

Perhaps historian John Keegan went too far in saying the Serbian conflict "proved that war can be won by air power alone," but if he was wrong, it was only in phrasing or word choice. Certainly Russian intervention played a leading role, as did the ever-growing land component that slowly surrounded Serbia. However, let there be no doubt. While air power was not in and of itself decisive, air power was the *most decisive* factor in ending the war and the Serbian atrocities occurring in Kosovo. Indeed, NATO's gradual approach and incremental increase in using air power, in conjunction with other means, ended the conflict. NATO did not win by air power alone, but would not have won without it.

In closing, Operation *Allied Force* achieved its goal. The ethnic cleansing and the massacres stopped. Historian Dan Haulman noted, "It ended one of the worst instances of genocide in a century of genocide." Hundreds of thousands of ethnic Albanians returned to their homes in Kosovo. Yugoslav and Serbian forces withdrew from Kosovo. The threat of the Serbian military to these people was at an end. While air power played a significant role in getting Milosevic to capitulate, the overarching success of *Allied Force* should always be measured by the ending of the atrocities. Just as important, perhaps leaders in other countries took note of NATO's strong resolve, its willingness to meet a humanitarian crisis with military force. NATO's united front, its allied force, reverberated well beyond the borders of Serbia to an entire European continent and around the globe.

Coalition losses during *Allied Force*		
Aircraft	Event	Aircrew
F-117	Shot down by SAM	Rescued
F-16CJ	Shot down by SAM	Rescued
AH-64	Crashed during training sortie	Two crew killed

FURTHER READING

Aronstein, David C. and Albert C. Piccirillo. *HAVE BLUE and the F-117A: Evolution of the "Stealth" Fighter*. Reston, VA: American Institute of Aeronautics and Astronautics, Inc., 1997

Bacevich, Andrew J. and Eliot A. Cohen. *War Over Kosovo*. New York, NY: Columbia University Press, 2001

Brown, Craig. *Debrief: A Complete History of U.S. Aerial Engagements 1981 to Present*. Atglen, PA: Schiffer Military History Press, 2007

Cordesman, Anthony H. *The Lessons and Non-Lessons of the Air and Missile Campaign in Kosovo*. Westport, CT: Praeger, 2001

Daalder, Ivo H. and Michael E. O'Hanlon. *Winning Ugly: NATO's War to Save Kosovo*. Washington, DC: The Brookings Institute, 2000

Haave, Christopher E., and Phil M. Haun, eds. *A-10s Over Kosovo: The Victory of Airpower Over a Fielded Army as Told by the Airmen Who Fought in Operation Allied Force*. Maxwell Air Force Base, AL: Air University Press, 2003

Hacker, Barton C. *American Military Technology: The Story of a Technology*. Baltimore, MD: Johns Hopkins University Press, 2006

Hinen, Anthony L. "Kosovo: 'The Limits of Air Power II.'" *Air and Space Power Journal*. May 2002

Kaplan, Robert D. *Balkan Ghosts: A Journey through History*. New York: St. Martin's Press, 1993

Lambeth, Benjamin. *The Transformation of American Air Power*. Ithaca, NY: Cornell University Press, 2000

Lambeth, Benjamin. *NATO's Air War for Kosovo: A Strategic and Operational Assessment*. National Book Network: 2001

Laslie, Brian D. *The Air Force Way of War: U.S. Tactics and Training after Vietnam*. Lexington, KY: University Press of Kentucky, 2015

Mijajlović, Mihajlo S. and Djordje S. Aničić. *Shooting Down the Stealth Fighter: Eyewitness Accounts of Those Who Were There*. Yorkshire, UK: Air World Publishing, 2021

O'Connor, William B. *Stealth Fighter: A Year in the Life of an F-117 Pilot*. St Paul, MN: Zenith Publishing, 2012

Olsen, John Andres. *Airpower Applied: U.S., NATO, and Israeli Combat Experience*. Annapolis, MD: Naval Institute Press, 2017

Olsen, John Andres. *A History of Air Warfare*. Dulles, VA: Potomac Books, 2010

Paget, Steven, ed. *Allies in Air Power: A History of Multinational Air Operations*. Lexington, KY: University Press of Kentucky, 2020

Rich, Ben R. and Leo Janos. *Skunk Works*. New York: Little, Brown and Company, 1994

Shaw, Robert L. *Fighter Combat: Tactics and Maneuver*. Annapolis, MD: Naval Institute Press, 1985

Warden, John A. *The Air Campaign: Planning for Combat*. Washington, DC: National Defense University Press, 1988

INDEX